PSYCHIC EXPERIENCE FOR YOU

A fascinating study of the many forms of psychic ability, with
practical tests and exercises for their development.

PSYCHIC EXPERIENCE FOR YOU

Rodney Marsden

THE AQUARIAN PRESS
Wellingborough, Northamptonshire

First published 1983
Second Impression 1984

British Library Cataloguing in Publication Data

Marsden, Rodney
   Psychic experience for you.
   1. Psychical research
   I. Title
   133.8   BF1031

ISBN 0-85030-368-0

*The Aquarian Press is part of the
Thorsons Publishing Group*

Printed and bound in Great Britain

Contents

Introduction

Psychic ability is normal, not supernatural. This book is designed to convince you of that. To be convinced, you may need the proof of thorough scientific investigations – I have provided descriptions of such experiments. Alternatively, you may need techniques you can try for yourself – I have also included many of those. This means that to enjoy this book you do not have to believe in psychic ability (nor necessarily disbelieve). All you need is an open mind and a willingness to learn.

Most people tend to think that psychic skills are arcane and esoteric. Nothing could be further from the truth. We all have a mind – we can all learn to be psychic. Incidentally, to describe a person as 'psychic' implies nothing more than that they have the ability to control and use certain mental faculties which are latent in all of us.

The key to using these psychic abilities lies in a lessening of your involvement with information being fed to your brain from the 'normal' sense organs (eyes, ears, touch, taste and smell receptors). Instead, you learn to stop and attend to your inner psychic sense as and when it is necessary or desirable to do so.

There are plenty of psychic techniques to try: telepathy, clairvoyance and precognition; dowsing; divination; healing; and so on. Later in the book we shall see the difficulties which science has in explaining psychic ability, and I shall suggest how these difficulties may be overcome. But let us first turn our attention to the mind and what it can do.

1.

Telepathy, Clairvoyance and Precognition

We can all obtain information with our minds. When that information comes from another mind, we are using telepathy. When we obtain information about objects, events or situations which could not have come from another person's mind, we are using clairvoyance. And, most extraordinary of all, if our minds were to obtain information about events which have not yet happened, we would be experiencing precognition.

These three psychic abilities are often discussed together under the label of extrasensory perception (ESP). This emphasizes the fact that our everyday, normal sense organs do not play a part in the psychic world. Truly, ESP is the 'sixth' sense!

As we shall see, there are easy and simple techniques which everyone can use to develop their psychic ability. We shall look at these in a later chapter. First of all, however, I want to describe some scientific experiments which have been conducted with people to demonstrate whether or not they have psychic ability. If you doubt the existence of ESP at the moment, these experiments will go a long way towards changing your attitude. If you already believe in ESP, I hope this chapter will still be interesting. If it does nothing else, it will reinforce your belief.

Together with these scientific accounts, I have included some anecdotes of how ESP can act in everyday life rather than the laboratory. Comparison of the scientific experiments and anecdotal cases is especially interesting because it allows us to make some important deductions: first, the conditions demanded by scientists for controlled tests can be artificial and unnatural; second, perhaps psychic ability comes much more naturally to a person who is relaxed and self-motivated; third, our psychic ability may be used in many different ways.

Telepathy

The first serious scientific attempts to investigate psychic techniques were made in the 1930s at Duke University, North Carolina, when Dr J.B. Rhine established a department for psychical research.[1] Rhine used a series of simple tests to try and detect psychic ability in his experimental subjects. As we shall see, the results which he obtained constitute good evidence for the existence of telepathy, clairvoyance and precognition.[2]

Rhine's work was based on the use of a special pack of cards – a Zener pack. This consists of twenty-five cards. There are five designs in the pack (circle, wave pattern, square, star, cross) and each card bears a single design on its face. Thus each pack is made up of five complete sets of cards. In the first tests for telepathy, Zener packs were shuffled and handed to one person, who was termed the 'agent'. The agent slowly turned the cards over and looked at each one in turn. As he did so, a second person (termed the 'recipient') tried to guess which design the agent was looking at. Clearly, the experimental design is crucial. The recipient must not be able to see either the agent or the pack of cards. This prevents him picking up any clues to the design on each card as it is turned over. He must, however, be sure when each card has been turned. And, of course, the results must be open to analysis in a way that proves beyond question whether or not some psychic faculty has been involved. In fact there are many suitable statistical techniques to do this. They are used to compare the number of times that the recipient would (in theory) be expected to guess the card correctly with the number of times that he actually did so.

The probability of guessing each card correctly is one in five. This is because there are five designs in the pack in equal numbers. Thus random guesswork would produce an average of one in five (20 per cent) accuracy; anything above that should be examined very closely, because it may indicate that the recipient was using his psychic ability to pick up information telepathically from the agent. This would enable him to identify the card correctly even though he could not see it. To make the interpretation of these statistical analyses as easy as possible the conclusions are usually expressed in terms of the probability of obtaining a particular score of correct 'guesses', or calls, by sheer luck or chance. The higher the number of correct calls, the lower the probability that the score was obtained by chance. (In familiar terms, we would express probability as 'odds'.)

With tests like these, Rhine obtained incredible results. His subjects often scored way above expectations, sometimes obtaining results which would be expected to arise by chance only once in about every million tests. (Or, to put it another way, results at a level of odds of more than a million to one against chance.) It would be pointless to try and discuss the statistics here. The essence of them is that over hundreds of thousands of tests, two definite trends emerge: first, some people are exceptional and score very highly, say eighteen correct calls out of twenty-five on one or two tests; second, others work only slightly higher than five out of twenty-five, but do it so persistently that their results just cannot be ignored.

What flaws might there be in these tests? Many scientists attacked the accuracy of the statistical analysis. However, in 1937 the American Institute of Mathematical Statistics issued a statement which vindicated Rhine. They stated that 'if the investigation is to be attacked, it must be on other than mathematical grounds'.[3]

Another objection could be that the design of these experiments was not really conducive to telepathy. After all, they involved long and boring tests with little personal interest to keep up the morale of the subjects. Yet, oddly enough, this really supports the results, because under such conditions, it is remarkable that telepathy was demonstrated at all!

Most of the objections to these tests actually resulted from the fact that in the 1930s the climate was not right for such revolutionary ideas as experimental investigations into telepathy. Opinion became divided between the supporters and believers on one hand and the critics – often trained scientists – on the other. Many of the latter group were abusive and ill-informed in their criticism. Fortunately, there were some scientists who made fair and rational objections to the techniques. This allowed the experimenters to modify and develop their tests until they had fulfilled all the conditions necessary to give their work a powerful authority. For example, the recipient was prevented from picking up information about the cards through watching the agent by excluding the possibility of any communication between them.

There were many other similar refinements of technique. Despite this approach, however, objections are still being raised. Professor John Taylor, in his book *Science and the*

Supernatural, writes: '. . . it is hard to accept the data, based as they are on the laborious piling up of tens or even hundreds of thousands of guesses to magnify a supposedly real but very small effect.'[4] But the validity of Rhine's work is later grudgingly admitted by Taylor, when he writes: 'The hypothesis that initial success is purely by chance . . . could only be made to stick if there had been incorrect use of statistical assessment. This had been discussed by Rhine, who notes, I think correctly, that "This hypothesis . . . is easily recognized as . . . denials of the efficacy of the mathematics of probability".'[5] Such attitudes are often held by those who do not believe in the reality of ESP. I think it is pointless to spend time and energy trying to devalue experiments which were the first serious scientific attempts to demonstrate the existence of telepathy — experiments which have stood the test of time.

There was, however, one fundamental objection to these first tests. You may have realized that even if the score of correct calls is well above chance, this does not *necessarily* prove that the recipient was using telepathy. He might have been using a clairvoyant faculty to predict the fall of the cards. If this was actually so, he would get them right whether they were turned over by an 'agent' or by a machine. Rhine therefore extended his work to investigate clairvoyance; we shall return to this shortly.

More recent work on telepathy has been carried out by Dr Thelma Moss (Assistant Professor of Medical Psychology) and Dr J.A. Gengerelli (Professor of Psychology) at the University of California.[6] They also used an agent and recipient, although they called them 'transmitter' and 'receiver' respectively. The investigation did not use cards, either. Instead, the transmitter was shown pictures which had been chosen for their strong emotional content. This was done because Dr Moss had noticed that spontaneous telepathic contacts often seem to occur when two people experience strong emotions. The tests were conducted as follows. The transmitter was seated in an isolation booth, where the pictures were displayed on a screen facing him. The chosen scenes included Nazi concentration camp victims, naked women, men on the moon, the Madonna and Child, and so on. Each scene was accompanied by suitable music, so as to reinforce the impression made on the transmitter. After each session, the transmitter recorded his impressions on audio tape; this provided an unalterable record of his feelings during the experiment.

The receiver was seated comfortably in a separate room about seventy-five feet (twenty-two metres) away. While the transmitter was looking at the pictures, the receiver was told to relax and relate any thoughts which came to mind; these were also recorded on tape. After each session, the tapes recorded by the transmitter and receiver were compared – the occurrence of similar expressions or phrases is good evidence of telepathy. But additionally, the receiver was shown a number of photographs arranged in pairs. In each pair there was one of the pictures which the transmitter had been viewing. Now, we would expect the receiver to guess correctly 50 per cent of the time – after all, there are only two choices for each scene. But a success rate greater than 50 per cent is almost certainly the result of telepathy.

Over a large number of trials, Dr Moss and Dr Gengerelli obtained some very interesting results. People who believed that they had ESP ability guessed correctly at a rate which represented odds of 3,000 to 1 against chance. This may not sound very much, but the results of many orthodox scientific experiments are regarded as acceptable if they show odds of only 100 to 1 against chance. But, perhaps more importantly, Moss and Gengerelli also found that people who did not believe they had ESP ability (or who did not believe in the existence of ESP) scored no better than the average expectation of 50 per cent. We shall come across more examples of this effect in other areas of psychic work; the implication is that *belief* is an important aspect of success in psychic work.

These investigations were later developed and gave even more impressive results. For example, tests were conducted with twenty-two transmitters in Los Angeles and fourteen receivers in Sussex University, England. The same procedure, involving the use of emotional scenes, led to results at the same level of success – with odds of 3,000 to 1 against chance. This time, however, some neutral or non-emotional scenes were used: and the score then showed absolutely no evidence of telepathy. As in the original experiment, the receivers' impressions were recorded onto tape and later compared with the pictures which the transmitters had been shown. In many cases, there were remarkable resemblances. For example, a picture of astronauts and rocket ships shown in Los Angeles elicited these comments in Sussex: 'Outer space with a ship heading for the moon'; 'I can see the world as if I'm in a space ship ... I'm in a cabin where everything is floating'; '. . . the use of satellites and flying platforms'. This is unlikely to be a coincidence, because references to space ships did not appear in any other experiments. Therefore we have yet more proof that telepathy actually exists. There are some other conclusions we can make: that telepathy is independent of distance; that an emotional scene (or more correctly, the emotional involvement of the participants) promotes or facilitates contact; and that belief in telepathy does indeed seem to be essential for success in experiments of this kind.

But the experiments show more than all that! They actually tell us something about the nature of telepathic communication. The point here is that telepathy does not necessarily involve clear communication from one mind to another. The receivers in these tests sometimes seemed to be 'interfering' with the impressions they received of the pictures. In one case, a woman receiver referred to hearing the music from *My Fair Lady* and a feeling of calmness when the Madonna and Child was being displayed to the transmitter. In another case, a receiver mentioned the Swiss Alps, little boys and ice creams when a picture of Disneyland was being transmitted. What may be happening is that the receiver is 'processing' the images in his subconscious or conscious mind after he has received them. This is called 'primary process distortion' and is actually fairly common during psychic work.

These experiments were generally well conducted, and the results satisfactory. Unfortunately, no attempts were made to investigate either the effects of different conditions on the facility of transmission or the nature of primary process distortion. Fortunately, other workers have developed techniques to tackle these problems. Possibly the most important of these is the 'Ganzfeld' technique.[7] This is a German word which means 'all-field', adapted here to imply a uniform field of information surrounding the senses of the receiver. The receiver wears eye shields which allow only a diffuse pink light to pass through, and his hearing is restricted to a background of white noise (this is a mixture of frequencies which sounds somewhat like the rush of distant water). The experiment commences only when the receiver is relaxed, so that internal distractions such as tension, worry and stress are also avoided.

One of the first people to use the Ganzfeld technique for telepathic transmission and reception of information was Charles Honhorton, a medical centre worker in New York. On one occasion, he was working with a nurse called Ellen Masser, who had reported spontaneous psychic experiences. With Masser under Ganzfeld conditions, a transmitter was shown slides of night clubs in Las Vegas. The commentary recorded by Ellen Masser included the following remarks: 'I am floating over some sort of landscape; it's surrealistic; a night club on 72nd Street. And marquees, night club marquees . . . just seeing night club marquees in Las Vegas.' Not unnaturally, when the experiment was finished, and she was shown the transparencies which the sender had been looking at, she exclaimed: 'It's fantastic! I can't believe it!'

Ganzfeld work is now widespread. When Charles Honhorton combined his results with those from ten other establishments, he calculated that their overall success rate showed odds of over 100,000 million to one against chance.

Kit Pedler gives an account of how he participated in some Ganzfeld experiments in his book *Mind Over Matter*.[8] After he had rid himself of the temptations to intellectualize and to create mental images, he found that impressions halfway between mental images and language descriptions formed in his mind. They seemed to come from a part of his mind that he 'had not previously been aware of'. One of the pictures which he was attempting to receive was a cluster of black witches' hats on a group of women. His commentary recorded during the 'receiving' period was along the lines of: 'Black saw tooth pattern like an old wood saw. All slopes, triangular slopes pointing upwards.' Obviously there is a clear similarity between the target and impressions received, although primary process distortion is taking place to some degree. In another test he accurately identified the silhouette of a palm tree halfway up a mountain. These experiments were well conducted and are very convincing evidence of telepathy. They go a long way towards dispelling the doubts of complete sceptics, and they reinforce the belief of those who already think telepathy exists. Such reinforcement is occasionally necessary; after all, the thought that we can 'tune' into someone else's mind is somewhat disturbing!

As the climate of opinion changes, more and more trained scientists are beginning to investigate all forms of psychic experience. Most of these researchers cannot be accused of errors in technique or faulty analysis of their results. Two such scientists are Dr Russell Targ and Dr Harold Puthoff, who worked at the Stanford Research Institute for seven years on yet another technique to demonstrate telepathy.[9] The procedure they used is called 'Remote Viewing'. Once again, a group of receivers are seated together. This time, however, they are trying to describe a location which is being visited by the other people taking part in the experiment (the transmitters). There is a complex experimental procedure which is designed to eliminate the possibility of fraud. About 100 sites are identified by map references; each site reference is placed in a sealed envelope. An independent observer picks one envelope at random and hands it to a driver, who departs with the transmitters. He opens the envelope only when he is well away from base. Meanwhile, the receivers have been locked into a room with another observer. No collusion is possible between the transmitters and receivers before the test begins and the possibility of fraud is therefore ruled out. At a prearranged time, the transmitters begin sending back signals about the site and its location. They do this simply by relaxing, looking around themselves and making good contact with the ground and objects in the vicinity.

Meanwhile, back at base, the receivers make two records of their impressions. First, they draw anything which comes to mind. Second, they record a commentary on a tape recorder. The idea is to prevent 'wishful thinking' when the transmitters bring back photographs of the site to compare with the impressions of the receivers. (Although I have simplified the technique, this is an effective and impressive way of demonstrating telepathy. There are complete instructions on page 82, if you wish to try this yourself.) As in all telepathic experiments, the first impressions of the receivers are the most important. After the experiment has been proceeding for some time, primary process distortion begins to affect the results. And, as you might expect, better results are obtained when the transmitters and receivers are confident about their telepathic ability and the receivers are relaxed and quiet. The results are not always correct – but I hardly think one could expect that. Overall, the results show a statistical significance – there is significant correlation between the transmitters' location and the receivers' impressions. What are we to make of it?

The results were published in *Nature*[10] (a highly respected scientific journal), and the result was very heavy criticism in great detail. As Kit Pedler has emphasized, this is an entirely normal part of the scientific endeavour, and once these criticisms have been met, the work is accepted by rational scientists. Targ and Puthoff answered the criticisms and went on to write a book about remote viewing in which they rebut other possible criticisms of their work.[11] Apart from such reasonable and fair criticism, there was also 'a crop of vindictive, irrational, and often extremely silly attempts to ... diminish their status and integrity as people'.[12] Other groups have continued work on remote viewing and their results are, broadly speaking, similar to those of Targ and Puthoff. From all these experiments we can see that the most likely deduction is that people's minds are able to communicate.

Scientists are reluctant to accept the idea of psychic ability because the concepts involved seem to break the scientific laws which they believe govern our whole existence. As we have seen, a lack of belief seems to affect people's success in creating telepathic contacts under experimental conditions; presumably the same applies to spontaneous telepathic contacts. In other words, we would expect most accounts of spontaneous telepathic experiences to be reported by those who have no scientific reputations or prejudices to consider. This does indeed seem to be the case. While I was writing this book, a series of bizarre events and coincidences began to develop; I interpreted them as spontaneous telepathic communication. For example, at one point I required information on brain wave physiology which did not seem to be immediately to hand. My choice seemed to be either to visit a reference library or carry on with a different subject. Putting the problem aside, I went out to lunch with a friend, a date that we had arranged some time previously. Jane was waiting for me when I arrived, and before I had a chance to say more than 'hello', she presented me with an article which contained all the information I needed about brain waves! When I expressed surprise, she told me that she had read the article and thought I might be interested in it. Because I had not mentioned my interest in the subject, it seems most likely that some kind of unconscious telepathy was going on. Possibly Jane had picked up my thoughts in some way without either of us deliberately attempting to establish contact. In passing, we should note that the fact Jane had this information at the exact time I needed it may also be some kind of psychic event. This is covered in Chapter 13.

On another occasion, I established what was quite clearly a telepathic contact, but again without any conscious intention to do so. I had agreed to accompany a friend on a car rally as his navigator. It was my first attempt at this sport, and I was more than a little apprehensive. On the day before the event I realized that I needed to obtain more information about the time we were starting, and I thought to myself, 'I must speak with David; perhaps I should phone him.' Even as the thought crossed my mind, the telephone rang. When I found I was speaking to David, I was, to say the least, surprised. When he informed me that he 'had had a feeling that he should ring me', my astonishment increased. (Even those who believe in ESP are often surprised or shocked when these events occur!) Now, on the face of it, this might all be coincidence. By that, I mean that one could perhaps regard all these events as totally unrelated. But when you begin to practise and develop your psychic ability, the 'coincidences' start to mount up, until there is no doubt in your mind that your psychic faculties are involved.

Sometimes one event has a profound effect on a person's attitude and beliefs about ESP. Professor Sir Alister Hardy is a marine biologist who has dedicated himself to the study of psychic events and religious experiences in recent years. But he has believed in telepathy, clairvoyance and precognition for many years. In fact, it was as long ago as the First World War when he experienced the event which left him in no doubt about the reality of telepathy. He was stationed on the Lincolnshire coast where he met a woman called Wedgwood. The officers sometimes visited her house for tea. On one such occasion, Mrs Wedgwood said quite suddenly and unexpectedly (I have paraphrased this somewhat from the original), 'Oh, I can see your brother quite clearly. He is in Germany in his prison camp; he is in a little room with a bed. He is sitting at a table drawing what I think must be some engineering plan; I can see him painting little squares of red and blue on a large sheet of paper.' Now, this was in fact what Hardy himself had been doing all afternoon, although no one knew it. He had been asked by his commanding officer to make a plan for use in a talk on battle strategy. It was that same afternoon that he had had the idea of cutting out red and blue squares to represent the opposing armies. He had done this in his billet – a bare room with a camp bed in it. Immediately he had finished, he went to the Wedgwoods' for tea, so no one could have told her what he had been doing before he arrived. Hardy had, however, mentioned some time before that his brother was a prisoner.[13]

There are many more anecdotes like this; you will probably

have had similar experiences yourself. Although these accounts provide only circumstantial evidence in support of telepathy, together they build up to an inescapable conclusion: telepathy is real – and not uncommon. They also remind us that telepathy does not usually involve direct verbal communication between two minds; it is not a faculty which enables you, shall we say, to discuss the week's events at a distance with a friend. Normally, spontaneous telepathic contact is likely to involve only an ill-defined feeling or emotion in our conscious minds. Clearly the implication is that if we were able to cultivate the conditions in which telepathy occurs, then it would be much more controllable. The idea of telepathy on demand is an attractive one. And, as we shall see, it is also a realistic one.

Before we move on to clairvoyance and precognition, a word of caution is in order. Telepathy is a subtle technique which can easily be confused with other psychic abilities. It is important to be sure that any unexplained contacts, communications and coincidences really are telepathic. A rarely quoted study by Alister Hardy proves this point. He was trying to demonstrate, once and for all, that telepathy was very common. To do so, in 1967 he assembled a group of 200 people to act as transmitters and twenty to act as receivers in Caxton Hall, London. The receivers were trying to 'read the minds' of the transmitters, who were viewing target pictures and objects. Using careful procedures to eliminate fraud, he obtained good results, with very high odds against chance.

So far, so good. He then conducted a series of control tests, in which he assembled groups of pictures at random. The idea was to see how pure chance compared with the results which he had obtained. What happened was shocking: the randomly assembled pictures seemed to be grouped together with a correlation greater than that in the telepathy experiments.[14] The reason for this is remarkable. Under appropriate conditions, objects and events can be brought together to appear in our lives as 'coincidences'. This is another psychic phenomenon which is discussed in Chapter 13. For the time being, we need only bear in mind that telepathy is but one of many psychic influences at work in our lives.

Clairvoyance

Do you ever know, with complete certainty, details about an

object or event when there is no way in which you could have obtained that information? That is clairvoyance: the passage of information to your mind when it is not possible for that information to have originated in another person's mind.

The original publication from J.B. Rhine's department at Duke University, *Extra-Sensory Perception*[15], contained a great deal of information on clairvoyance. This was because Rhine had adapted his techniques so as to counter criticism of his experimental design. In doing so, he built an automatic card shuffling machine, which could lay a card face downwards with no human involvement. Clearly if a subject was able to guess the design on the face of the card, telepathy could not be the explanation. The answer had to be clairvoyance. (You might now be wondering how telepathy can ever be demonstrated in this kind of experiment. In fact, it is comparatively easy; you merely ask one person to think of a card and ask another to 'guess' what is in his mind. Exactly the same kinds of statistical analysis can be applied to these results.) Rhine obtained the same successful 'above chance' results whatever design of experiment he used. And there, in one matter-of-fact statement, we have proof of the existence of clairvoyance! But let us see what other points we can make about this extraordinary psychic technique. First of all, clairvoyance is a difficult word to define. You may like to consider the technique of dowsing (water divining) at this point. Suppose you walk across a field with a dowsing rod and succeed in finding water. You might be more ready to accept your success than you would be if you were told that you had scored highly on a clairvoyance test. Yet in both cases you are using a very similar faculty or ability. You are obtaining information about your environment – information which you are unlikely to receive telepathically – by the use of your psychic ability. The point is this: a mere name can affect people's attitudes towards psychic events and procedures. To overcome this an open mind and a willingness to try to suspend
. your disbelief are important.

Second, some writers use 'clairvoyance' as a generic term for all psychic techniques. This is, however, only a matter of opinion, and not very important. In fact, this point is only significant if you demand proof that clairvoyance is a real faculty, distinguishable from telepathy and precognition. Consider the following example: suppose I suddenly know that tomorrow I will receive a phone call or letter from one particular person. Is that clairvoyance, or can it be ascribed to telepathic communication with the writer or caller? There is no way of knowing, and similarly in only a few series of experiments can the total absence of any other mental influence be 100 per cent proven. Rhine's work was one such series; another was the work of Dorothy Martin and Frances Stribic at the University of Colorado between 1938 and 1940.[16]

Under controlled conditions, Martin and Stribic asked their subjects to guess the order of cards in shuffled Zener packs. One subject, 'C.J.', guessed the design of cards in 110 packs at an average rate of 8.17 correct calls per pack (remember the result expected on average is five). His calls were then compared with the order of cards in other shuffled packs. This comparison acted as a control – no psychic ability was being used. When compared with random packs, the calls which 'C.J.' had made showed almost exactly the figure one would predict: 5.02 correct per pack. Clearly, this is powerful evidence for clairvoyance.

Precognition

Precognition is not the same as prediction. To predict is to foretell or prophesy. Often the word has no connection with psychic techniques; predictions can be based on reasoning from past knowledge or experience. But, in a psychic sense, prediction refers to some specific procedures which provide knowledge of future events. Examples are the *I Ching* and other systems of divination. Precognition is generally said to have occurred when a person has gained some knowledge of future events quite unexpectedly – with no intention to do so. This is what the word means – 'fore-knowledge'. In a later chapter I shall show how you can increase the frequency of precognitive insights to your own advantage by using a dream control technique.

Precognition covers a variety of experiences. As I have hinted, the most important are precognitive dreams. They are probably also the most common type of precognitive experience. Another type is what can loosely be termed a 'vision': that is, a scene flashing through the mind as though you were watching a film. These tend to occur during moments of altered states of awareness during the daytime (this is explained in Chapter 3). The third type of precognitive experience is a non-visual one. For example, if you had a sudden feeling of certainty that a particular event was going to happen at some point in the future, that would be precognitive. Often such feelings concern unfavourable or tragic events: they are then called premonitions or presentiments. It is my belief that many hunches and intuitions are actually precognitive psychic experiences. I have known several businessmen who attributed their success in business decisions to psychic fore-knowledge. But whatever the type of experience precognition is generally unexpected and unintended.

An individual who has had a precognitive experience often needs no more proof of the reality of psychic ability. I know one woman who woke in the middle of the night and said to her husband, 'Something awful has happened to one of the children.' Later she received a phone call from the police to confirm that an accident had occurred. Precognitive experiences often make a deep and long-lasting impression on people. Even the less serious ones are astonishing enough. But, once again, caution is in order. Consider the following example. A friend of mine experienced what he thought was precognition one day as he arrived home from work. As he walked in through his front door, he had an overwhelming certainty that his wife was going to tell him some bad news about a mutual acquaintance of ours. Sure enough, when he met his wife, she told him about a court case involving some serious charges levelled against this person. It seemed unlikely that he had known about this before, because the matter was quite unexpected, and a big surprise to all of us. When I heard about this, I decided to try and find out whether precognition was really involved. I travelled home on the train with my friend next day. What I believe had actually happened was far removed from precognition; he appeared to have subconsciously read the image of a newspaper headline reflected in the train window, even though this was upside down and inverted.

John Taylor gives a similar example in his book *Science and the Supernatural*.[17] He relates how he often reached out to pick up the phone on his desk just before the bell rang. Only after this had happened many times did he realize that the phone gave an almost inaudible click just before ringing. That was what had subconsciously registered, and so caused him to reach out before the bell began to ring. I think that the lesson in these two anecdotes is that we should always be careful not to assume that the most appealing explanation (precognition) is necessarily the correct one. Let us now examine some more anecdotal cases of precognition, keeping this note of caution in mind.

Perhaps the classic case of precognition is Abraham Lincoln's dream of his own assassination. Shortly before he died, he related these details to Ward Lamon, US Marshal for Columbia at the White House, who recorded them in his diary:

> About ten days ago, I retired late and began to dream. [I dreamt] that I left my bed and wandered from room to room, seeing no-one, but all the time hearing people sobbing as if their hearts had broken. I determined to find the cause, so I went on to the East Room where, to my surprise, was a platform with a covered corpse on it. 'Who is dead?' I asked one of the soldiers. 'The President,' he replied. 'He was killed by an assassin.'[18]

Dr Thelma Moss gives an account of how a cancer research student telephoned her laboratory and asked if he might meet her to discuss what he believed had been a precognitive dream.[19] He arrived carrying a large picture drawn by his sister after she had had a violent dream. In her dream she had seen herself in the front seat of a car moving along a freeway. Suddenly, a car travelling in the opposite direction had crashed across the central reservation and smashed into her car. The left front wheel had flown into the air and changed into a skull. All these events were represented in an emotional way in the girl's drawing. Now, here is the interesting, yet tragic, part of the story. The student reported that two weeks after this dream, all the events had actually happened. His sister had been travelling in a car; it had been hit by one coming the opposite way, and the left front wheel had flown off and landed some distance away. The girl had been killed instantly.

Another such example was related by Dr J.B. Rhine's wife, Louisa.[20] One day, she had a vision of her elder son Hubert lying dead in the bath. As any mother would, she kept a special check on him while the vision continued to haunt her mind. Two years later the premonition 'came true'. As she dressed to go out, she heard Hubert singing and whistling. Held back by her innate fear, she suddenly realized that he had become quiet. Forcing open the door, she found him overcome by fumes from the gas heater. There is no doubt that he would have died if she had not acted in the way she did.

What should we make of this? What faculty is being used to foresee the future? Why do these dreams, visions or flashes of knowledge occur without warning or without any intention to produce them on the part of the subject? Can we even accept the existence of precognition in a framework of knowledge which includes our concepts of time? If we are looking at events which have not yet happened, how is the information reaching us? Does this not imply that our lives are running to a predetermined course? Alternatively, does it mean that we can use dreams like this to alter our actions and so prevent disaster (as Louisa Rhine did)?

In later chapters, the answers to most of these questions will become clear. I shall also suggest how the occurrence of precognitive dreams can be increased. There are examples of precognition in which a person has learned of good fortune, rather than tragedy. But there is no doubt that, for good or bad, to control precognitive dreams could be very useful. But before we look at ways of doing just that, we must first examine some scientific research.

To test for precognition, one really needs something which is completely random. For various reasons it is difficult to be sure that any sequence of events is not part of a larger pattern. For example, on my desk as I write is a small device which has eight neon bulbs linked by circuitry in such a way that they flash on and off, apparently at random. You certainly could not consciously detect any pattern or sequence just by watching the bulbs flashing. But here, as so often, appearances are deceptive. The bulbs are arranged in the circuitry so that each time one flashes, it affects the state of charge of all of the capacitors in the circuit. And since this is the variable which affects the rate of flashing, each bulb has an effect on all the others. It turns out that the flashes form a rather complicated sequence. Thus we can see that in designing equipment to test precognition there is an inherent danger of using a predetermined series of events. If this was the case, the subconscious mind might be able to detect the sequence. Correctly foretelling which event will occur next is then hardly demonstrating precognition.

The nearest thing which we have to the truly random event is the decay of radioactive atoms. Although radioactive material as a whole has a known half-life (time taken for half the material to decay), the actual decay of each radioactive atom is unpredictable. Dr Helmut Schmidt has invented a machine which uses the unpredictability of this event as a test for precognition.[21] Briefly this is how his machine works.

All the time it is switched on, an electronic circuit drives a counter through four positions in the sequence 1–2–3–4 –1–2–3–4, and so on, at very high speed. Each counter position is connected to a corresponding lamp. When the counter is stopped, the lamp corresponding to the position it has reached will light up. Next to each bulb is a push button. Any of the four buttons will stop the counter, but not by switching off the counter directly. The buttons activate a circuit linked to a radioactive compound in such a way that the very next radioactive decay after the button is pressed will stop the counter. Thus, after pressing any button, there will be a completely indeterminate and unpredictable delay before the next decay occurs. When the decay occurs, the counter stops immediately and the lamp corresponding to that position lights up. Obviously if the button which a person presses to stop the machine corresponds to the light which comes on when the counter stops, we may assume precognition is at work. But to be sure of this, a subject must score more than one in four (25 per cent) correct – this being the probability by chance.

In one series of tests, a subject tried 7600 button presses and was 27.2 per cent correct. This is outstanding. Statistical anslysis shows that under such circumstances, a 27.2 per cent success rate would arise by chance only once in every 100,000 trials, each consisting of 7600 presses! An even longer series of tests produced results at a level of odds of 4,500,000 to 1 against chance. Though this seems very convincing, there is a drawback. It may be that psychokinesis, rather than precognition, is at work. If a subject can affect the equipment with his mind, he may be able to stop the counter at a particular point. Schmidt took account of this by refining his equipment. He adapted the machine so that a paper tape with 100,000 digit codes punched in it would control the sequence of the counter. This is a fixed relationship, and the only way a subject could predict the next lamp to light would be by using his precognitive faculty. The results obtained were still at a level well above chance – conclusive proof of precognition.

All the experiments described in this chapter are of interest and reinforce one's belief in the reality of psychic work. But it is the anecdotal cases which may have more relevance for most of us. After all, we experience ESP in our daily lives, not in a laboratory. The two approaches combine, of course, and you can adapt the scientific techniques for your own use. In a later chapter I shall demonstrate how you can do this.

REFERENCES AND NOTES

I have assumed that most readers of this book have neither the time nor the resources to search out obscure journals. In general, therefore, I have listed only the most accessible references.

1   The establishment of this department is described in J.L. Randall, *Parapsychology and the Nature of Life* (Souvenir Press, London, 1976), chapter 5.
2   Comprehensive descriptions of Rhine's work can be found in Randall, op. cit., and Thelma Moss, *The Probability of the Impossible* (Routledge and Kegan Paul, London, 1976), pp. 119–22.
3   Reported in Moss, op. cit., p. 121.
4   J. Taylor, *Science and the Supernatural* (Maurice Temple-Smith, London, 1980), p. 51.
5   Ibid., p. 51.
6   Moss, op. cit., pp. 179–83.
7   For a lucid description of Ganzfeld work, see K. Pedler, *Mind Over Matter* (Eyre Methuen, London, 1981), pp. 52–66. Also M. York, *Research in Parapsychology* (Scarecrow Press, Metchuen, New Jersey, 1976).
8   Pedler, op. cit., pp. 58–66.
9   Pedler, op. cit., p. 31.
10 R. Targ and H. Puthoff, 'Information transmission under conditions of sensory shielding', *Nature,* vol. 251, pp. 602–7.
11 R. Targ and H. Puthoff, *Mind Reach* (Granada, London, 1978).
12 Pedler, op. cit., p. 35.
13 A. Hardy, R. Harvie, A. Koestler, *The Challenge of Chance* (Hutchinson, London, 1973).
14 Ibid., pp. 1–118.
15 J.B. Rhine, *Extra-Sensory Perception* (Faber, London, 1935).
16 For a comprehensive account of such experiments, see G. Mishlove, *The Roots of Consciousness* (Random House, New York, 1975).
17 Taylor, *Science and the Supernatural,* op. cit., p. 74.
18 Reported in J. Pratt, *Parapsychology: An Insider's View of ESP* (Doubleday, New York, 1964), p. 148.
19 Moss, op. cit., pp. 198–9.
20 Reported in Taylor, *Science and the Supernatural*, op. cit., p. 149.
21 The most accessible account of Schmidt's work is contained in: Randall, op. cit., pp. 123–35. But see also H. Schmidt, 'Mental Influence on Random Events', *New Scientist,* 24 June 1971, p. 757.

2.

Psychokinesis: Mind Over Matter

Of all the psychic techniques described in this book, it is psychokinesis (PK) which has attracted the most widespread attention. This is not surprising for, after all, the thought that we can cause physical objects to move about or to bend and break by means of mental effort alone is an astounding one, with far-reaching consequences for our concepts of mind and matter. But all this attention has caused more fraud and deception than is found in any other psychic field. (This, in turn, has done a great deal to discourage investigation into psychic work by scientists.) So I start this chapter with a warning – do not believe everything you read about PK, nor, for that matter, everything you see.

Professor Arthur Ellison, who is Professor of Electrical Engineering at London University, demonstrated the value of that warning at a recent lecture. Towards the end of the lecture, he asked members of the audience to participate in an experiment in levitation.[1] They were told to concentrate on a bowl of flowers on a table, willing the bowl to move upwards. While they did so, Ellison played a tape recording of a Buddhist meditation chant – ostensibly to help the audience concentrate. What happened next astounded the sceptics and believers alike. As they concentrated, the bowl of flowers began to move, finally lifting a few inches off the table! What would you conclude? What *could* you conclude? Obviously, but almost unbelievably, that levitation had taken place. However, this conclusion would be quite wrong. The tape recording was played so as to disguise the noise of electromagnets hidden under the table. These repelled magnets in the flower bowl and caused it to move upwards: the whole thing was a stage trick, in fact. But had you not known this, you would probably have concluded that the experiment really demonstrated PK. In other words, you simply did not have enough information to assess the real situation. You should apply this cautious attitude to any other account you may hear or read anywhere – even the ones in this book. For example, I have obtained my information from other books and original references which may already be inaccurate. (As it happens, the experiments and events described in this book are all well authenticated, but the principle is important.) So if you read that some psychokinetic activity has taken place, the question which you should have in your mind is: 'What would I ask to make certain that it really happened?' Perhaps another example will help the reader to see what I am getting at.

Some years ago, Uri Geller made several television and radio broadcasts in Britain. He demonstrated how he could apparently bend spoons, stop watches and even repair defective clocks just by using the power of his mind. After each of his radio and television features there were literally hundreds of claims from one end of the country to the other that objects had bent or twisted and that clocks had stopped or started while he was on the air. For example, on 23 November 1973, Geller broadcast live on a BBC Radio 2 programme. One man from Dunstable reported: 'Our radio was on in the lounge while Uri Geller was bending the spoon. I walked into the kitchen and found that two teaspoons on the draining board were arched out of shape. Later I found half a dozen knives in a drawer all with a noticeable curve in the blade which just wasn't there before. It's unbelievable.' A woman from Middlesex said that she was stirring soup with a ladle when suddenly, 'My hand twisted, and I felt the ladel moving and cracking. I was petrified. I pulled it out of the soup, and all the enamel had been broken off by the distortion of the ladle.' In Guernsey a whole family joined in the mass experiment that Geller was holding. They held a broken alarm clock, a wristwatch that had stopped ticking, a fork and a screwdriver, but nothing happened. Later, however, when they returned home after an outing, the watch was ticking, and the fork, placed in the kitchen, 'curled up within five minutes'. There are many more reports like those, which can be found in *The Search for Psychic Power* by David Hammond.[2] What does it all mean?

You may say that the sheer volume of these circumstantial reports constitutes some valuable evidence in favour of PK. My answer to this would be: 'Did you personally see an object move?' And consider this: would you believe your best friend – your husband or wife, even – if they told you that an object had twisted out of shape while Uri Geller claimed that he was bending a spoon by the power of his mind in a radio studio? I do not think you would. So how much reliance can be placed on reports from people we do not know in situations we cannot see? But let us leave aside the question of the specific reports which poured in after Geller's radio and television broadcasts, and consider the general reliability of anecdotal accounts of psychic events.

When individuals experience events which might possibly be suggestive of something they would like to believe in, they are predisposed to jump to the wrong conclusions. For example, those who believe in UFOs see an unexplained light in the sky and assume it must be a spaceship from another world. Those who experience a series of trivial coincidences assume there is a psychic force at work. Those who notice a bent spoon for the first time after a psychic has appeared on TV assume that he must have bent it. In reality the sad fact is that although such stories are amusing, they cannot help us to decide objectively whether PK is real or some figment of a willing imagination. Fortunately, a few scientists have been brave enough to risk the opprobrium of their colleagues by investigating PK in their laboratories.

The value of such objective testing was illustrated by a demonstration of how a conjuror might imitate a psychic. Kit Pedler, on a British television programme, showed how he could straighten a piece of wire by stroking it. Or at least, 'that is what it looked like'.[3] In fact the wire was made from Nitinol, a special alloy which returns to the shape in which it was forged when subsequently heated. A straight piece of this wire can be bent by hand and then held surreptitiously in a stream of hot air. It will 'mysteriously' straighten out. Another metal alloy melts at a very low temperature. By making, let us say, a spoon from this substance, it is possible to bend and break it with very little effort. There are good reasons here for making a strenuous effort to repeat metal bending experiments under laboratory conditions where no trickery is possible. The two most notable investigators in this field have been Professor John Taylor of King's College, Cambridge and Professor John Hasted of Birkbeck College, London University.

John Taylor was a guest on the first British TV programme to feature Uri Geller. The events which he witnessed were so incredible – while apparently authentic – that he resolved to look into the matter further. In his book *Superminds*, Taylor describes experiments which he conducted, chiefly on Uri Geller, but also on several individuals who came forward with claims of paranormal abilities after Geller's TV appearances.[4] Taylor's chief concern was to avoid the possibility of fraud. Many sceptics, from magicians through journalists to scientists, had dismissed Geller as a skilful conjuror. Indeed one magician, the 'Amazing Randi', has written a biography of Geller which lays emphasis on the fact that he was once in court in Israel on a charge of deception, after claiming that a conventional two-person code routine in a night club act was a demonstration of ESP.[5] (This fact obscures Geller's still unexplained later abilities.) Taylor believed that his experiments were as sound and rigorously controlled as any conventional scientific test. He describes experiments in which pieces of metal contained within glass and wire mesh tubes were bent or twisted by his subjects. In his words: 'I have personally witnessed the Geller effect under conditions in which fraud can be completely ruled out.'[6] One of the tests which led to this conclusion involved a small crystal of lithium fluoride sealed inside a plastic container. Geller held his hands over the container without touching it at any time. The crystal broke within ten seconds. Professor Taylor described this as 'devastating'. As he remarked, he had placed his own hands between Geller's and the container so that no direct manipulation was possible.[7] There is an interesting sequel to this research.

Between 1975 and 1980, Taylor's belief in what he calls 'the supernatural' evaporated. His book *Science and the Supernatural* is devoted to proving that psychic work is 'impossible'.[8] The theme that runs through the book is something like: 'Paranormal metal bending and ESP break existing laws of science, therefore they cannot exist. Because they do not exist, I do not believe in them.' Taylor claims that he had been too ready to accept faulty experimental procedures and evidence from other scientists which did not exclude the possibility of fraud or inaccurate reporting. He describes a later series of tests with Uri Geller in the following way:

> He came to our laboratory for one and a half hours. In spite of the very friendly atmosphere he did not succeed at all during that period. Nor has he returned to be tested again . . . in spite of several warm invitations . . . As far as I am concerned, there endeth the saga of Uri Geller; if he is not prepared to be tested under such conditions his powers cannot be authentic.[9]

To be fair, Professor Taylor admits that this about-face could be ascribed to his desire to counteract the hostility and opposition of his colleagues to his experiments on the 'supernatural'. But he denies this, simply stating that he was not careful enough about the conditions by which he judged the work. The whole story is a disappointing one. My own impression is that the case made out in *Superminds* for the reality of psychic effects is stronger than the case against in *Science and the Supernatural*. What went wrong? I concur wholeheartedly with Lyall Watson, who has written of John Taylor:

> I find his current stance, in his rejection of the phenomena and his return to the orthodox field, no reason for rejoicing. In his position, with academic status to defend, it is clearly more politic to be seen to be gullible than to be considered unscientific ... John showed great courage in pushing the investigation as far as he did, but I can't believe his mind is easy even now he has denied it thrice ...[10]

There is perhaps another aspect to all this. Taylor was unable to explain what he had discovered in terms of existing scientific concepts and knowledge. At the beginning of *Superminds* he outlined the rationale behind his work thus: 'Either a satisfactory explanation must be given for Uri Geller's phenomena within the framework of accepted scientific knowledge or science will be found wanting.'[11] Because this proved to be impossible, he rejected the whole field. Yet we cannot be sure that the knowledge of science is yet complete, so how can this be sufficient reason to dismiss psychic techniques? All in all, an investigation which initially set out, in the words of Stan Gooch, to 'save the marvellous paranormal baby from being thrown out with the bathwater of lies and deceit', leaves us no further forward. There is one small point which emerges clearly, though. Uri Geller's first work with John Taylor was very successful. His subsequent work was not. This notorious unpredictability of psychic work has been seen many times in scientific investigations. I think it happens because the psychic is both sensitive to, and influenced by, the opinions of those around him. Thus, if John Taylor wanted the first set of tests to work, but not the second, then that is probably exactly what would happen. This means Taylor's work does little more than confirm the importance of the psychic having belief in his own ability (this does not apply so much to spontaneous psychic experiences).

The main reason why I have introduced the inconclusive work of Professor Taylor is that we can learn something from the stringent tests which he now applies to accounts of PK. His discussion of Uri Geller in *Science and the Supernatural* forms a background by which all psychic work may usefully be judged. For example, he mentions several tricks which might provide an explanation of Uri Geller's metal bending abilities.[12] I leave it to the reader to decide whether they do in fact do so. They are:

(1)   *Substitution:* an already bent object replaced one being worked on while the audience's attention was distracted. But Geller did not know what objects he would be asked to bend and his work was frequently videotaped.

(2)   *Alteration:* mechanical force applied to an object might have been used to bend it when the audience was distracted. Although some subjects who claimed to have paranormal metal bending ability did use force to bend metal objects, measurements in Taylor's laboratories showed that Geller himself applied only a fraction of the force required to bend an object mechanically.

(3)   *Chemical:* there are chemicals which alter the structure of metal, but they are highly corrosive and poisonous and easily absorbed through the skin. Not a likely suggestion.

(4)   *Heat:* a high temperature could twist a metal object but would also destroy human tissue. No one suggests this method was ever used in public demonstrations.

(5)   *Mass hypnosis of the audience:* clearly a ludicrous suggestion. You cannot hypnotise a group of people *en masse*.

(6)   *Inaccurate reporting:* obviously this is a possibility. But it applies to *all* investigations by scientists and journalists, not just those into the psychic world. And there is no reason to suppose that a higher proportion of cheats are found amongst scientists investigating ESP or PK than amongst those working in any other field of research.

Let us now turn our attention to the work of Professor Hasted, who has always maintained a firm belief in the reality and existence of paranormal metal bending. Professor Hasted conducted his investigations in a cubicle screened against electrical fields or electromagnetic radiation in Birkbeck College. (This was only one of several precautions taken to ensure that the best possible results were obtained.) A piece of metal was connected to a strain gauge (a device to measure any movement, no matter how small) and placed on a table in front of the subject, who was not allowed even to touch it. An identical strain gauge not connected to any metal acted as a control and showed up any spurious deflection or signal in the recording apparatus. Professor Hasted collected a large body of evidence which shows that his subjects could indeed bend metal by the power of their minds alone.[13] Kit Pedler later interviewed one of the younger individuals whose psychokinetic abilities had been investigated by Hasted. The boy described the state of mind which was necessary for success in these terms: 'There's very little physical sensation, but it's certainly important for me to be in a relaxed state of mind. It doesn't work very well when I try to concentrate.' He confirmed that the effect happened when he turned his mind away from it, as if it 'catches him out'.[14]

To place this section further into perspective, I must quote what John Randall has written:

> ... the danger comes when ... enthusiasts begin writing and arguing as though the whole case for the reality of psi [that is, psychic events] rests upon the honesty and integrity of Mr Uri Geller ... the case for psi does not depend upon any one individual, no matter how much publicity he receives in the media. The case for psi rests upon the fact that the same phenomena have been witnessed, over and over again, in many different subjects and by many different experimenters.[15]

Psychokinesis refers to a wide range of events; obviously, by definition, any event where physical objects are influenced by the human mind alone. So metal bending need not be the only test of PK. You can, for example, try to influence the fall of dice – we shall consider this later in the chapter. Some readers will have come across Russian work on PK with the famous psychic Nelya Mikhailova (known also by her maiden name of Nina Kulagina). This woman realized she was psychic during the Second World War, when she was in hospital recovering from an injury. One day when she was very angry she was walking towards a cupboard when a jug moved to the edge of the shelf, fell off, and broke.[16] After this, she was plagued by poltergeist activity (discussed later). There have been many extraordinary claims about her abilities. For example, it has been said that she can shift objects placed on a table top just by willing them to move. However, this is not a convincing demonstration of PK, because it is difficult to distinguish between movements which really are caused by PK and those which are merely the result of electrostatic forces. (A person can sometimes generate an electric charge on his or her hand – or an object – and then induce it to move small distances.) Much of Mikhailova's work – and incidentally that of others like her – can be explained in this way. But there is little doubt that she has a real and extraordinary psychokinetic ability. One test in particular which proves this is so was conducted by Genady Sergeyev, a neurophysiologist at Leningrad. First of all, an egg was broken into a tank of salt solution. Mikhailova then concentrated on the egg, and with a great deal of effort – separated the white from the yolk. The whole event was recorded on film.[17]

Another line of evidence very suggestive of the reality of PK is the phenomenon of rapping and levitation which occurs in spiritualist and psychic meetings. Although I do not accept that spiritualists conjure up discarnate spirits, there is good evidence that unexplained movement of objects is a common feature of such meetings. The question is whether these effects stem from trickery or really represent PK.

In considering the answer to this question, we shall examine one of the most well known examples of the phenomenon.[18] The long and complicated story began when members of the Toronto Society for Psychical Research were investigating a haunted house. Several people who were in the basement of this house agreed that they had seen a 'ghost' – although they tended to regard this as a 'thought form' produced by the mental activity of the individuals present. If this were so, they reasoned, it might be possible deliberately to create another such thought form to a description of their own choosing. For convenience, let us refer to this thought form as a ghost. (I am not suggesting that this has any connection with the spirit of a dead person.)

This group of people met regularly for over a year with the intention of producing their ghost. In order to reinforce its reality in their minds, they constructed a detailed history for it. They called the ghost Philip, and decided that he had lived in the 1600s, had been married to a girl called Dorothea, and had had a gypsy mistress named Margo. The idea of building up the history of a ghost in this way and then seeing if some manifestation of it could be produced seems crazy. After all, ghosts and spirits are generally thought of as really being connected in some way with past history, whereas Philip was pure invention.

Nevertheless for a whole year the eight members of the group held weekly meetings at which they meditated and spent some time discussing, drawing, and further embellishing the life history of Philip. Nothing happened. At this point, one of the individuals, who had been researching in the psychic field, discovered a traditional technique for generating psychokinesis. The group adopted this technique in the hope that it would assist with the development of their ghost. They stopped meditating and began to be more relaxed together, laughing and establishing a good rapport. On the third and fourth sessions after they had changed technique they felt and heard raps on the table around which they were all sitting. At this stage, each of them thought that one of the others was kicking the underside of the table. Eventually it became clear that this was not the case and one of the group asked the table if it 'was' Philip. They adopted a code of one rap for yes and two raps for no: the table indicated 'yes'. Subsequent questions about Philip's life also produced psychokinetic knocks. Sometimes the answers were such that Philip's life story had to be modified to take account of them.

Now, let us review what has happened so far. A group of people established psychokinetic effects by means of a technique which involved a good group rapport in a light-hearted atmosphere. (We know that the table rapping must have been psychokinetic because sound waves are generated by vibration; and when vibration occurs for no good reason in an otherwise normal object, PK is clearly indicated.) This is our first mystery. The group did not consciously set out to obtain psychokinetic effects: they simply wanted to generate a ghost. It seems that the psychokinetic effects were produced by the traditional psychic technique which the members of the group had adopted. The group then seem to have used the psychokinetic noises as a means of expressing their subconscious ideas about 'Philip'.

Shortly after the psychokinetic knocking had begun, the table began to move around the room, apparently of its own accord, although members of the group were resting their hands lightly on its surface. This is our second mystery. Judging by the original account of the work, there can be little doubt that the table movement actually took place. What is difficult to accept at first is that members of the group were not simply pushing it. However, the table moved on either one, two, three or all four of its legs. This fact alone excludes the possibility that members of the group were physically moving it: you cannot balance a table on one of its legs and move it across a room simply by touching the surface – even if there are eight people involved.

To the sceptic, this all seems absurd. How could a group of people produce psychokinetic effects just by behaving in a light-hearted way? Experienced psychics tell us that this table-moving technique is very well known. Admittedly the group of eight individuals described here were not experienced psychics. On the other hand, they had a very strong desire for some psychic phenomena to occur; they could also rationalize the actual psychokinetic effects as being a manifestation of their 'thought form' or ghost. Indeed, these effects appeared in a manner which conformed to the conditions they had already described and which were uppermost in their minds – their ideas about Philip's life story. If you wish to try a similar technique, you can find the method in *You are Psychic*[19] by Sophia Williams.

Let us now return to a more general discussion of PK. I wish to consider an aspect of PK which causes more problems than any other: poltergeist activity. Poltergeists are not the same as ghosts, although they are frequently confused. This is how I understand and use the terms. 'Ghosts' look like living beings. Usually, each one has the form of a man or woman – sometimes an animal – known to be associated with the history of a particular place. Yet they have no real existence in our physical world; they seem to be nothing more than mental perceptions. We know this because not all the people in a group will see a ghost at the same time. In fact, ghosts literally 'occur' when a man or woman in a particular state of consciousness momentarily experiences a kind of historical clairvoyance – a precognition in reverse, as it were. This involves sensory input from the psychic sense and not from the eyes, although the process of perception seems to be the same in both cases. The result is that the person momentarily 'sees' an event or figure which really did exist in history upon that spot.

Poltergeists, on the other hand, are very real, in the sense that events described as 'poltergeist activity' do actually occur in the physical world. But poltergeist activity is not caused by physical beings, spirits or ghosts. It is a result of the activity of an individual's psychic faculty. To understand this more clearly, we can examine some typical accounts of poltergeist activity. Such accounts are generally well documented, and amongst the most significant cases which have been reported there has never been a single proven instance of fraud. Although most poltergeist activity is pointless, some seems downright destructive or harmful. As will become clear, this is because such activity often represents the release of repressed hostility. (Incidentally, the occasionally malevolent nature of the phenomenon has unquestionably led to the traditional explanation of poltergeists as being the work of mischievous elves, goblins and ghosts.)

The first case which I shall describe occurred in December 1967 and early 1968 in the offices of a lawyer (one Herr Adam) in Rosenheim, Germany.[20] He suffered much interference with his office furniture. For example, the fluorescent light tubes turned through ninety degrees and exploded, the photocopying machine leaked fluid when no one was near it, the telephone rang or lost connections in the middle of calls without apparent reason, and the telephone exchange mechanism registered phantom calls to the speaking clock. Not surprisingly, a thorough inspection of the electricity and telephone systems was ordered. F. Karger and G. Zicha, two physicists from the Max Planck Institute of Plasmaphysics in Munich, were called in to investigate.[21] They fitted a power station recorder onto the mains supply in the lawyer's office and later also set up equipment to monitor magnetic field changes. They also recorded the sounds which formed a part of the poltergeist effects. At this stage these were thought to be caused by voltage fluctuations in the electricity supply. But measurements with all this equipment – assuming that it was unaffected by the poltergeist – quickly ruled out electrical and magnetic effects as the cause of the problems. Despite (or perhaps because of) all this attention the disturbances continued, so Herr Adam suggested that an emergency generator be used to supply electricity. The suggestion was implemented, but the problems continued. At this point, someone noticed that fluctuations in the recording apparatus seemed to occur especially when a nineteen-year-old girl, Anne-Marie S., was present. For example, the first interruption of the electricity supply, as measured by deflection on the electrical recording apparatus, occurred when she arrived at work in the morning; and when light bulbs shattered, the pieces flew towards her.

When asked for his opinion, the director of the Institute of Parapsychology at Freiburg University suggested that Anne-Marie was indeed the most likely cause of the phenomena. It is said that Herr Adam joked to Anne-Marie, 'The only things that haven't moved are the pictures on the wall,' whereupon one tilted through a complete circle! Later, Anne-Marie left the office and transferred to another lawyer's practice; significantly, the poltergeist activity went with her.[22]

It is a curious but well documented fact that poltergeist activity of this sort nearly always occurs in the presence of an adolescent – usually (but not exclusively) a girl. And it has been observed that such girls are often unstable, unhappy and emotionally disturbed. By all accounts Anne-Marie had an unhappy childhood and suffered from great emotional disturbance including irritability and frustration. Clearly such states of mind may be a natural part of adolescence.

Another famous case also took place in 1967, in the United States.[23] When a writer on psychic affairs was being interviewed on a Miami radio station, the owner of a local business called to ask how he could remove a poltergeist which was breaking beer mugs, ashtrays, vases and other crockery. The writer, Sue Smith, went along to the scene of the disturbances – which turned out to be a warehouse – with a film crew. Over the twenty-four hours they were there, objects flew around in such profusion that trickery was absolutely impossible. Because the effects continued while the investigation was being conducted, great care was taken to note the positions of all the people in the warehouse when objects were flying around. It seemed fairly obvious from these observations that a nineteen-year-old shipping clerk called Julio Vasquez was responsible. He was never caught throwing objects, but there was fairly clear evidence that he was the centre of the disturbances. For example, the incidents stopped when he left the building. They also decreased in frequency with increasing distance from him – rather like the way in which the intensity of shock waves falls off as one gets further away from the epicentre of an earthquake. A psychologist who conducted personality tests on Vasquez found that he was an unstable individual with serious feelings of self-doubt and inadequacy.

The third case is a more recent one. On the day I write about poltergeists, my local newspaper carries an article entitled 'Haunted Holiday Homes Riddle'.[24] This article describes a series of unexplained events in the home of a family living in Blackpool, England. The family concerned bought a building which they decided to modernize and convert into holiday flats. While the work was being carried out they lived in private accommodation in the same building. Soon after the work had begun, however, mysterious events started to happen. 'Footsteps' and 'movements' were heard in the building; the family and guests 'sensed a presence'; ornaments were flying across the room; and so on. It is suggested in the article that the cause of these disturbances might have been the activity of a 'spirit'. And, curiously enough, a woman died within a few feet of the building after falling out of an aircraft overhead in 1935. Obviously it would be easy to accept a connection between these two events. The reaction of the family was to call on the services of a Catholic priest to bless the 'haunted' rooms. Shortly afterwards, in the words of the lady of the house, 'We knew it was all over when half-way through the night we heard a tremendous bang on our bedroom door.' This occurred without any physical mark being made on the door (a case of psychokinetic noise very similar to the Toronto table rapping).

Unfortunately, six months later, the disturbances started again. This time a mirror crashed to the floor and objects moved around. We are, therefore, forced to look for an alternative to the 'haunted house' theory. This is because one would not expect 'spirits' – if they exist, that is – to appear intermittently.

I believe that the key to this affair lies in one particular sentence which appeared in the newspaper article. This is it: 'Two teenage daughters have reported beds being shaken violently by an unseen hand.' As on so many other occasions when poltergeist activity occurs, we have the presence of adolescent girls. It seems much more likely that either one or both of the girls were causing poltergeist activity than that the noises were produced by the activity of a spirit. Before we see how an individual might be responsible for such effects, we can briefly list the predominant characteristics of poltergeist cases. Most notably, one individual seems to be responsible in each case. This is fairly obvious: the phenomena stop when he or she leaves the area. The events also fall off with distance from that person. (Anne-Marie and Julio were typical in these respects.) But the person concerned is generally quite unaware that he or she is responsible – the phenomenon is truly subconscious.

Gauld and Cornell have recorded many cases similar to those of Rosenheim, Miami and Blackpool in their comprehensive book *Poltergeists.*[25] They also describe a series of experiments which they conducted to investigate the notion that some form of earth tremor or vibration lies behind poltergeist effects. They relate how they designed, built and tested a machine to shake buildings: needless to say, this was a futile exercise.

So the most obvious feature of these cases is that they are associated with a personality rather than a place. How could a person be responsible for the often alarming nature of poltergeist effects? In fact, it is conceptually no more difficult to answer this question than it is to explain how a person could be responsible for remarkable displays of metal bending. Therefore the easiest way of approaching the problem is to consider the nature of psychokinesis in general.

PK really is a case of 'mind over matter'. In common with psychic healing, it is a technique where matter is dramatically influenced by the human mind. This can happen in a variety of ways: metal bending; production of noises without any physical cause (compare the table rapping in Toronto with noises and bangs in the Rosenheim and Blackpool poltergeist cases); the movement of objects (which is the most common feature of poltergeists); the operation of mechanical systems without reason; deliberate attempts to influence the fall of coins or dice tossed from a shaker (which we shall consider in a moment); and so on. We might simplify the position by developing a system of classification. First, there are conscious attempts to cause PK phenomena. The majority of cases of metal bending fall into this category. Obviously any other occasion when someone deliberately sets out to affect matter with his or her mind also falls into this category. Second, there are subconsciously controlled examples of PK – predominantly, poltergeist activity. Within this classification we have all manner of variations: two particularly contrasting examples being Nelya Mikhailova's conscious concentrated attempt to move objects and John Hasted's metal bending youth who, conversely, cannot achieve any results when he concentrates. It is this diversity which leads me into another classification of PK effects; a classification which I believe is more important than the conscious/subconscious one given above. To illustrate this, I would like you to try the following experiment. Obtain a die and something in which you can shake it.

For the first part of the test, you should try to generate a lighthearted, joking, jovial atmosphere. You might like to ask some friends to join you: if they too have an interest in this field, it will help. Within this atmosphere of jollity and light-heartedness, you will throw the die several times with the intention of obtaining a particular face – say, five or six – as often as possible. Before you start, remind yourself that it is important you do well. While shaking and throwing the die, do not concentrate hard on the number which you have chosen, but casually remind yourself of it. You will probably have some considerable success in throwing the desired face of the die, especially on your first few throws. But do remember that the probability of obtaining each face by chance alone is one in six. So the total number of times you will obtain the desired face by chance equals one sixth of the total number of throws.

The second part of the experiment involves the same apparatus: die, or dice, and shaker. This time, however, you will consciously try to influence the fall of dice by directing your full energy and attention onto them. This is difficult to explain, but easy to understand when you have tried it for yourself. What you are doing, in fact, is diverting your attention from the action involved in throwing the dice onto the numbers you wish to come up. Having a mental picture of the dice lying that way up often helps considerably. However, the important thing is that you should expend considerable energy; that is, not physical energy in throwing the dice, but psychic energy on ensuring that they fall in a particular way. Be certain in your mind that you *will* obtain the desired result. You can do this by (forcefully and energetically) mentally repeating, 'I am going to get three sixes' – or whatever you want.

Now, this 'concentration' technique differs from the more 'relaxed' technique in several ways. Obviously the attitude of mind in which you start is different. But, more importantly, the way in which the techniques affect you are also quite different. There is no noticeable difference in the way you feel after a few minutes of using the relaxed technique. The concentration technique, however, is psychically (and physically) exhausting. If it works – that is, if you are putting enough energy in to make it work – you will only be able to sustain the effort required for a few minutes. After this, you will find that you are quite unable to influence the dice, and you will also feel mentally drained. It is not desirable to reach this state very often, so I have included the test for the sake of illustration only. There is a loose connection with the work of Nelya Mikhailova here. After her psychokinetic feat of separating the egg yolk and white as described on page 34, she was mentally and physically exhausted and looked haggard – like an old woman, as one observer put it. The same generally applies to anyone who moves objects using something akin to the concentration technique. It has to be said, however – and your experiments may well have convinced you of this – that the concentration technique is, at least initially, more effective than the relaxed technique in producing PK.

I believe that poltergeist effects may be caused by a release of psychic energy in the same way that occurs in the concentration technique. Associated, as they so often are, with individuals who have emotional problems, poltergeists may represent an uncontrolled discharge of hostility or repressed and transformed aggression. (Repression is a process whereby an individual does not consciously accept or express a particular emotion. But because the original cause of the emotion is still present in the subconscious mind, emotional energy will build up until a process of transformation takes place and the emotion is finally expressed in a quite different form.) The implication of this idea is that repressed hostility – or other emotional states – have an energy substrate which can be transformed into an energy capable of moving objects at a distance. We can call this 'psychic energy'. The fact that poltergeist activity is usually subconsciously controlled (at least, its occurrence is not consciously intended) supports this theory: repression of emotions from consciousness usually produces some form of subconsciously determined effect. The most common are psychosomatic illness, irritability and depression. In this special case, I am suggesting that repression leads to a transformation of emotional energy into the psychic energy which causes PK. No draining or exhaustion effect occurs in the people responsible for poltergeists because they have a reservoir of emotional energy on which to draw. Suggestively, when their environment – in the widest possible sense – changes, and their emotional problems come to an end, the poltergeist activity also ceases. Excess emotional energy may be a natural part of human development, but only a few individuals ever show signs of poltergeists. It would, however, be very interesting to know how many unreported cases of poltergeist activity actually occur!

To sum up: although poltergeist effects are usually subconscious, and the dice throwing concentration technique is a conscious process, they probably have a similar underlying psychic mechanism. Both these procedures contrast sharply with cases of PK such as the Toronto group's table rapping and movement, the Geller metal bending effect, and the relaxed dice throwing technique. Such cases conspicuously do not involve a draining of energy from the subject. Indeed, they often revitalize the individuals concerned. Thus, from these observations, we are forced to conclude that this group of cases does not involve the same mechanism as the concentration technique. There are good reasons why this conclusion is likely to be correct. For example, when we examine psychic healing, we shall find parallel effects: one method of healing is draining, the other is not. And it is true that some people find dowsing a tiring procedure, while others do not. Jean Burns has suggested that many people naturally use a method which falls midway between the concentration and relaxed techniques.[26] This probably explains why there can be such variation in people's personal experiences during psychic work.

Let us now return to a more general consideration of the issues involved. When trying to influence the fall of dice by PK, it does not seem to matter whether or not the dice bounce against another object before coming to rest. This observation has led Jean Burns to suggest that the ability to obtain a particular face on a die is not PK, but a kind of precognition.[27] In other words, the subconscious can identify the particular moment at which the die will fall the desired way up when you release it. I was at first tempted to accept this explanation. However, several observations make me feel it is not correct. First, the movement of the table by the Toronto group was conducted in a light-hearted environment and was unquestionably psychokinetic. Therefore, we know that PK effects can occur in a relaxed atmosphere. So why should dice throwing not be truly psychokinetic? Second, I have watched various individuals influence the fall of dice from a mechanical shaker which released them at random times. The dice were made to fall with a particular face upwards a significantly greater number of times than would be expected by chance alone. Clearly, precognition could not be at work here.

As you might expect, the results of the relaxed technique are generally much less significant if you are in an irritable or upset mood when you try it. (This applies to all aspects of psychic work.) And when trying to use either the concentration or the relaxed technique, it is better if feelings of self are not predominant. As we shall see, this is because such feelings involve a state of consciousness quite unsuited to psychic work. In the next chapter, I shall explain the ways in which you can develop your psychic ability by learning to control your state of mind or level of consciousness.

As a demonstration of the effectiveness of the exercises described in the next chapter, you should try a test for PK twice. First of all, do it now, following the instructions given below. Record your results. Then read Chapter 3, try the exercises described there, and afterwards repeat the test. Record your second set of results and compare the two. The comparison should reveal a significantly greater success rate the second time around. However, do remember that this is not a precise test of PK ability. The need for repeated throws of coins in the absence of electronic equipment makes the test susceptible to boredom. Furthermore, the results are of no scientific value because of the limited number of throws involved. It is only intended to be a demonstration of the fact that there *are* ways of learning to develop your psychic ability.

A test for psychokinesis
In the following test, your aim is to influence the fall of a normal, unbiased coin. You may choose to try and make the coin fall heads or tails upwards. The greater the number of throws, the more reliable the results will be; so it will help if you can obtain the assistance of a group of friends. For successful results, you need to pick people who believe in PK but who will not fabricate the results. If you are working in a group, you can pool your results and probably obtain up to 1000 throws of the coin. If you are working alone, you need to throw the coin at least 100 times for the results to have any meaning at all. Of course, you do not have to do this in one sitting – short sessions are probably preferable. (Using two coins at once is also acceptable.)

An atmosphere of light-heartedness will help. You should throw the coin(s) from a cup or shaker, rather than your bare hands, onto a flat surface. You can re-read the instructions about the dice throwing technique on page 41, and apply them while you toss the coin. Each time the coin has come to rest, mark whether it landed heads or tails uppermost on a score sheet. Afterwards tot up your results and refer to the Appendix for the method of analysis and probability calculation. The comparison of your results before and after trying the exercises described in the next chapter can be set out here:

(1) Score before trying relaxation and visualization exercises: ... heads/tails out of ... throws

Odds against this being due to chance alone: ... to 1

(2) Score after trying the exercises: ... heads/tails out of ... throws.

Odds against this being due to chance alone: ... to 1

REFERENCES AND NOTES

1 This event is described in K. Pedler, *Mind Over Matter* (Eyre Methuen, London, 1981), pp. 13–14.

2 D. Hammond, *The Search for Psychic Power* (Hodder and Stoughton, London, 1975).

3 Pedler, op. cit., p. 80.

4 J. Taylor, *Superminds* (Macmillan, London, 1975).

5 Taylor, *Science and the Supernatural* (Maurice Temple-Smith, London, 1980), p. 114.

6 Taylor, *Superminds,* op. cit., p. 126.

7 Ibid., p. 160.

8 Taylor, *Science and the Supernatural,* op. cit.

9 Ibid., p. 118.

10 Reported in S. Gooch, *The Double Helix of the Mind* (Wildwood House, London, 1980), p. 238.

11 Taylor, *Superminds,* op. cit., p. 11.

12 Taylor, *Science and the Supernatural,* op. cit., pp. 115–17.

13 See J. Hasted, *The Metal Benders* (Routledge and Kegan Paul, London, 1981).

14 Pedler, op. cit., pp. 86–7.

15 J.L. Randall, *Parapsychology and the Nature of Life* (Souvenir Press, London, 1976), p. 186.

16 L. Watson, *Supernature* (Hodder and Stoughton, London, 1973), p. 138.

17 Reported in Watson, op. cit., p. 139.

18 The whole story is related in Iris Owen with Margaret Sparrow, *Conjuring Up Philip* (Harper and Row, New York, 1976).

19 Sophia Williams, *You Are Psychic.*

20 For an account of this and other poltergeists, see A. Gauld and A. Cornell, *Poltergeists* (Routledge and Kegan Paul, London, 1979).

21 Reported by A. Resch, 'The Rosenheim Case', *Journal of Paraphysics,* vol. 3, pp. 69–76.

22 Gauld and Cornell, op. cit.

23 See Gauld and Cornell, op. cit; and Thelma Moss, *The Probability of the Impossible* (Routledge and Kegan Paul, London, 1976), pp. 331–2; and also W.G. Roll and J.G. Pratt,

'The Miami Disturbances', *Journal of the American Society for Psychical Research,* vol. 65, 1971, pp. 409–54.

24   *West Lancashire Evening Gazette,* Blackpool, 22 January 1982.
25   Gauld and Cornell, op. cit.
26   Jean Burns, *Your Innate Psychic Powers* (Sphere, London, 1981), p. 172.
27   Ibid., p. 168.

3.

Learning to Use Psychic Techniques

The material in this chapter forms two distinct sections. The first consists of background information on the brain, the mind and the nature of consciousness. The second consists of exercises which form the basis of a system designed to increase one's ability to function psychically. So that you fully understand the material in the later part of the chapter, I recommend that you read the background information *before* trying the exercises. Nothing in what follows is complicated or difficult to understand.

The Brain, the Mind and Consciousness

A question which often arises when people begin to develop their psychic ability is: 'How do psychic events relate to our everyday consciousness?' To answer this, we need to consider the activity of the human brain and mind. We all intuitively realize that psychic events do not 'just happen'. Occasionally, of course, we spontaneously experience telepathy, or have a flash of insight that turns out to have been precognitive. Generally, however, such events are rare; they tend to occur only under unusual circumstances: when we are relaxed and daydreaming, for example, or perhaps when we are under a great deal of stress. Oddly enough, it is this observation which provides a clue to the nature of psychic experience. Psychic events tend not to occur during our normal, everyday, waking consciousness, but in *special states of consciousness*.

Let us digress here and consider what is meant by consciousness. It can be defined as 'that property of the mind which enables us to feel, perceive and think'; in other words, to be aware. Aware of what? you may ask. Well, aware of the world around us. Aware, also, of our own existence. And, indeed, aware of our own consciousness. Obviously this last statement is at one level tautological. Yet it sums up the problem precisely: how can we use our conscious thinking ability to analyse our own consciousness? Many of the philosophers and scientists who have approached this problem have begun by debating whether brain and mind are separate realities, whether mind is an illusion, or whether mind is a by-product of the brain's activity. Thus, for example, there are several possible explanations of why I am able to, shall we say, move my arm. Here are but two of the possible reasons:

(1) I decide to do so in my conscious mind. After I have made this decision, my subconscious mind (see page 50) transmits appropriate instructions to the nerve cells of the brain which control movement in that part of the body.

(2) On the other hand, I might be a machine which reacts automatically to certain stimuli in a certain way. If this is true, then a feeling of freedom or choice in the act of moving my arm is illusory.

I am happy to say that, at least for the present, we can avoid this question. It is not fundamental to our discussion, and we can merely note that the idea of man as a mindless automaton cannot be supported by rational argument. We can therefore assume that the mind of man has a real existence. However, we shall return to a closely related issue – whether man has an independent free will – in Chapter 11. For the time being the observations central to our discussion are these: the mind can work on several levels, and its activity is closely linked to that of the brain. Let us consider these points in greater detail.

When a person thinks or dreams, or even when just asleep, the brain is active. We know this because electrical impulses in the nerve cells of the brain produce a very small but quite distinctive pattern of electrical activity on the scalp and forehead. This activity can be measured on an electroencephalogram, or EEG. The EEG has shown that the electrical activity of the brain varies according to what we are doing. For example, during everyday life, particularly when the mind is directed to some problem or when anxiety and tension creep up on one, there are waves of electrical activity running from the back of the head to the front at anything between fourteen and twenty-two cycles per second. These are called beta waves.

Other well defined frequencies of brain waves include alpha, theta and delta.

Alpha waves are those with a frequency of between fourteen and seven cycles per second. They are common during moments of peace and calm, and during certain phases of dreaming and sleep. Theta waves extend down from seven to four cycles per second and occur in most people during sleep and briefly in the daytime when problems result in strong emotions or frustration. They are also associated with very creative periods. Finally there are delta waves, which need not concern us here because they occur only during the unconscious periods of deep sleep. Thus it is clear that, at least to a certain extent, brain wave activity changes according to the activity of the mind – in both consciousness and the unconsciousness of deep sleep. This is a key point in our discussion. Rather than try to define a specific state of consciousness in which psychic work can take place, we must turn to an analysis of brain wave activity and see if we can pinpoint any feature which is characteristic of psychic work. In fact, the changes in brain activity during psychic work are well documented.

The Russians were amongst the first researchers in this field. In March 1967 one of their research groups was conducting a test of telepathic communication between two men: Karl Nikolaiev in Leningrad, and Yuri Kamensky in Moscow.[1] Nikolaiev was the receiver, Kamensky the transmitter. Both men were wired up to EEG recorders. The researchers noticed that when Nikolaiev indicated he was ready to receive impressions, his brain was producing regular alpha wave activity. They described his associated mental state as 'relaxed but attentive'. A similar pattern of brain and mind activity was observed in Kamensky when he began transmitting. The most successful subjects of the experiments of Rhine, Moss and other research scientists also displayed alpha waves; the effect is, in fact, a general one which is seen in all kinds of psychic work. (There is some evidence, mainly from research on Nelya Mikhailova, that PK and perhaps one type of psychic healing involve the production of *theta* waves.[2])

All in all, then, the evidence points to one inescapable conclusion: psychic work takes place in a state of mind, or consciousness, characterized by brain wave activity of a frequency lower than normal. This conclusion raises an interesting question: are brain waves of the alpha frequency the cause of, or merely the result of, a particular state of mind? There is no clear answer to this question, but it is much more likely that externally measured brain waves are nothing more than a sign of underlying physiological mechanisms. In the words of Lyall Watson, 'It seems certain that both telepathy and psychokinesis occur only under certain psychological conditions and that these are the ones marked by production of a particular frequency.'[3] In other words, by learning to develop a state of mind in which alpha wave frequencies are dominant, you can develop your psychic ability. How is one to do this, though? By examining the nature of consciousness.

The most obvious division of the mind's activity is into its conscious and its subconscious aspects. By definition, subconscious processes are those which occur below the level of awareness. (Below is, in this sense, a metaphor. It is not used to imply a superiority/inferiority distinction between different aspects of the mind's overall activity. The term has probably arisen because the parts of the brain which deal with subconscious processes are physically located below the parts which deal with conscious processes.) Most routine body functions – breathing, temperature regulation, heart beat, and so on – are controlled by automatic regulatory systems of which we have no awareness. Memory, too, is a subconscious function. Additionally, all sensory input is processed subconsciously before being passed on to the conscious mind. Clearly it would be impractical for us to be aware of all our sensory impressions and memories during all our waking hours. So the subconscious acts as a filter and selects what may be important. This it presents to consciousness as required: for example, when we hear our name at a party in amongst the general background noise. Another obvious way in which the subconscious serves us is by working on problems while our attention is elsewhere: a name which one cannot recall pops into one's mind quite unexpectedly later on, and one 'sleeps on a problem' to decide what is best to do. The subconscious never stops working, even when we are asleep.

It used to be thought that the distinction between consciously and subconsciously controlled functions was quite well defined. Then bio-feedback systems proved that individuals could learn to lower their heart rate or relax muscles normally under involuntary, subconscious control. Indeed, one might have suspected that there was actually a gradation of consciousness extending from 'purely subconscious' to 'purely conscious'. Consider, for example, the following levels of mental activity:

(1)   dreaming – which must be conscious, otherwise one could not remember the content of dreams
(2)   'daydreaming' with one's eyes shut
(3)   'daydreaming' with one's eyes open
(4)   reading a whole page of a boring book without taking in a single word
(5)   performing a task while still aware of oneself or one's surroundings
(6)   being completely absorbed in a task, to the exclusion of all else
(7)   complex mental calculation, analysis or reasoning
(8)   abstract thought and creativity.

This is not intended to be a complete list of possible states, or levels, of consciousness; there are, no doubt, many more. (The 'lucid' dreams reported by many psychics are but one such example.) It is intended to show that consciousness is not an unvarying level of awareness. Nevertheless, all of us are familiar with the mental state in which we spend most of our time; and this is the nearest we can come to a definition of everyday consciousness. Here is an extract from the writings of the pioneer psychologist William James:

> ... our normal waking consciousness, rational consciousness as we call it, is but one special type of consciousness, whilst all about it, parted from it by the filmiest of screens, there lie potential forms of consciousness entirely different.[4]

The 'potential form of consciousness' with which we are presently concerned is the state of mind associated with the production of alpha waves by the brain. This is difficult to describe to someone who has not experienced it. Phrases like 'controlled awareness', 'concentrated passivity' and 'relaxed attentiveness' do not convey the true meaning. The most obvious characteristic of this 'alpha level' is that both mind and body are relaxed: tension produces beta waves, which disrupt the alpha needed for psychic work. Equally obvious is the fact that analytical and calculating thought disrupt alpha and produce beta. But despite this, it *is* possible to think at the alpha level if one reduces the conscious effort involved to a minimum. This is necessary for two reasons. First, the conscious mind is associated with sensory input and stimulation from the physical world, where ESP is a rare event. But, more fundamentally, the psychic sense – the part of the mind which receives and transmits information psychically – is normally beyond conscious awareness: it is subconscious. We only become aware of it, or at least make an approach to it, when we lessen the activity of the conscious mind to a minimum. Information can then pass into our awareness with very little disruption (although the problem of primary process distortion remains). At first, all of this seems like mere conjecture. However, it is correct. We know this because the use of a tool such as the dowsing rod, to display psychically received information, bypasses the conscious mind entirely – and the results, at least for a beginner, tend to be much more accurate.

Before we consider the exercises designed to develop psychic ability, there is another point which I should like to emphasize. Although normal conscious thought is reduced during psychic work, your conscious thoughts, feelings and attitudes can affect the results you obtain when acting psychically. This was clearly demonstrated in one series of tests conducted by Dr Gertrude Schmeidler in New York. She asked a group of students to fill in a questionnaire in which they were asked whether or not they believed in ESP. They were then given a standard clairvoyance test, which involved identifying the order in which randomized cards were turned over. The result was very clear: those subjects who believed in ESP achieved much higher scores than those who did not.[5] Now, because everyone can learn to be psychic, this can mean only one thing: belief in one's own ability is a prerequisite to success in the psychic field. Your first task, therefore, is to believe that you can be psychic. That is up to you.

To sum up what I have been saying: the development of the alpha state can provide a key to unlock the door to the psychic world. How are we to do this, though? Some people – perhaps ten per cent of the population – seem to spend most of their time in alpha naturally. (It is very likely that the successful subjects of the experiments described in the chapter on telepathy, clairvoyance and precognition all fall into this ten per cent.) Another group of people who show great development of the alpha state are practitioners of meditative disciplines such as Zen Buddhism and yoga. Not only can they slow their brain wave frequency down from everyday beta into alpha or even theta, but they can also maintain production of alpha for long periods. However, it takes months, if not years, to learn alpha production with these techniques. Moreover, as is well known, the devotees of these arts often withdraw from society to practise their skills. No matter how much we might like to do this, it is just not practical.

It is sometimes suggested that alpha is generated whenever a person shuts his eyes. Indeed, there are people who can practise telepathy and the other psychic skills discussed in this book just by closing their eyes and directing their mind to whatever they wish to achieve. However, for most people, shutting the eyes is not enough. This is because the great majority of people are too emotionally and physically tense (even with their eyes shut) to enable psychic impressions to pass from their subconscious to their conscious. Or, more specifically, the conscious mind is too alive with stress and worry to notice the subtle psychic impressions received by the subconscious. So alpha produced by the simple act of shutting the eyes remains 'scrambled' by everyday beta. To produce prolonged, pure alpha is a different matter altogether.

When one is physically relaxed in alpha, one tends to feel very calm and peaceful. Indeed, there are many real benefits associated with alpha. For example, the breathing rate slows down from the normal twelve breaths per minute to about six breaths per minute. The depth of each breath is also reduced. The heart rate, too, slows down. The implication of this is that the body is using less oxygen. Since oxygen consumption is a measure of the metabolic rate, the metabolism of the body must be slowing down. This happens because the anxiety and stress which make us all excited and overactive during normal life are cut out, thereby allowing a state of deep rest to develop. Often we are not aware of how much stress our bodies suffer during everyday life. Consider a car driver: he knows about the problems he experiences on a long journey. What he may not know is that his heart rate can shoot up to as many as 200 beats per minute because of the stress.

There are various systems available for training oneself to function in alpha which are primarily directed towards the benefits described above. One such system which is widely available at the time of writing is that popularized form of Eastern mysticism known as transcendental meditation, or TM for short.[6] TM is a simple and apparently very effective way of boosting one's alpha wave production during short periods of the day, so that the effects carry over into the remainder of the day's activities and thereby lower stress and tension. It is a useful way of controlling one's own mind and it has gained great popularity because of its effectiveness. However, as far as psychic work is concerned, the teachers of TM would be the last to claim that their technique is useful in developing your psychic ability. Although you may find yourself becoming more psychic if you take up the practice of TM, this is only because you are spending more of your time in alpha, and it is gradually 'spilling over' into the rest of your day. You cannot take your periods in alpha and use them directly for, say, telepathy. We need a way of producing the alpha state on demand, so that we can then use it for whatever psychic work is required. Importantly, there has to be no sign of this happening; in other words, our daily lives must not be affected.

At this juncture, an important point arises. Some readers may be slightly confused if they have read descriptions of the alpha state elsewhere. They may have read that one is not consciously aware in the normal sense while in alpha. What is the truth of this? Well, first of all, one is always conscious to a greater or lesser degree when one is in alpha. For example, dreaming during sleep involves the production of alpha waves. You can easily train yourself to remember your dreams, so you must be in a state of mind at least related to normal consciousness – if dreams were truly subconscious, you could not remember them at all. Normally, however, we are not aware of this dream con-sciousness; our minds are centred on the dream rather than an awareness of ourselves. I believe the same applies to the alpha state generated during TM. It is a form of deep relaxation in which dream-like thoughts pass through the mind. Such a technique is very effective in the relief of stress. However, there are ways of learning to function with full consciousness and awareness at the alpha level.

To differentiate between methods of alpha production like TM and methods where one is fully conscious, the former are termed *passive* meditations and the latter are termed *dynamic* meditations. (I use the word meditation in no sense other than to imply some technique for the production of alpha.) One par-ticular dynamic system I want to consider is the 'Silva Method of Self Mind Control', Silva or SMC for short. If you have access to one of the centres where Silva is taught, you may like to consider whether it appeals to you. It does not teach you anything you could not learn yourself, but it does teach it more quickly. One of the interesting things about Silva is that it acts, quite independently, as confirmation of the importance of alpha in psychic work. I shall describe their courses briefly before going any further.

The research which was the foundation of Silva began in the 1950s when José Silva, a Texan who owned an electronics business, but had no formal education, taught his children to relax in such a way that with vivid mental visualization they could learn much more effectively. What he was in fact doing, as we now realize, was training his children to go to a deeper level of mind corresponding with the alpha wave frequency. The most astounding thing happened on one occasion when his daughter was being questioned about her schoolwork: she answered a question before it had been asked – while it was only a thought in José Silva's mind, in fact. Clearly the training to go to alpha level had in some way led to the ability to experience telepathy. Although the development of a standard training course took thirteen years, it is fair to say that the experience gained over this time did lead to a simple, practical course which, in forty hours, can train anyone to develop alpha. The point is that everyone can learn to produce alpha waves and the particular state of mind associated with them. As José Silva writes in his book *The Silva Mind Control Method:*

> At the alpha level ... you cannot bring your feelings of guilt and anger with you. If these feelings intrude, you will simply pop out of the level. As time goes on, they stay away for longer, until one day they are gone for good. This means that those activities of the mind that make the body sick will be neutralized. This is the first step in mind control, and by itself it will go a long way towards setting free the body's healing powers and giving it back the energy squandered on tension.[7]

The most interesting claim made for Silva is the possibility of using the alpha state for any of the following: actually making an imaginary event into a reality (such as obtaining a new job, moving home, making money, making better relationships, even healing serious illnesses); telepathy; distant healing and diagnosis; speed learning; using dreams to solve problems; and making events occur just as you need them.

By the way, you may wonder why people do not remain in

alpha naturally, since this state is apparently so useful. The answer is simple. Alpha wave production starts in the creative part of the brain, a part which is overwhelmed by the emotional and reasoning part in the majority of people. As we have seen, emotions and reasoning in everyday life are conscious activities which elicit beta waves, and these swamp alpha (and theta). Training the creative side of the brain to be more active in producing alpha and theta waves does not stop the emotional and reasoning part working, but it does reduce its dominance. This is an interesting point which is worth considering at greater length.

Anatomically, it is clear that the cortex, or thinking part of the brain, is divided into a right and a left hemisphere. This has been known for many years. But the discovery that the human brain is also divided functionally is a comparatively recent one, made only after the development of brain surgery designed to cure a particular form of epilepsy. In this treatment, the huge mass of nerve fibres connecting the right and left hemispheres is severed. (The operation actually cuts about 200 million nerve fibres which connect corresponding areas of the two hemispheres.) Remarkably, the post-operative patient is apparently unchanged: memory, verbal ability and the feeling of self-consciousness are all retained. Careful studies on these patients have, however, shown that all is not as normal as it seems. They have also provided much information about the mechanism of the normal brain.

The first conclusion reached from such studies is that the left hemisphere alone is responsible for linguistic ability, verbalization and conscious experience. This has been worked out through the use of a neat quirk of neural anatomy. Nerves from the right and left halves of the human visual field go to the left and right hemispheres respectively. Now consider an individual who has undergone this surgery. Words can be flashed onto a screen in such a way that he can only see them in the right half of his visual field. This information is fed to his left hemisphere, as normal; but, because of the operation, it cannot be passed on to his right hemisphere. Nevertheless, each time a word is flashed on the screen, the patient has no difficulty in selecting the appropriate article from a selection of objects placed in front of him. But when words are flashed onto the left half of his visual field, his ability to select the correct object is greatly reduced. Similar tests have shown that the left hemisphere is also the dominant calculating and reasoning hemisphere.[8] This logical superiority has led to the left hemisphere being termed the 'dominant' hemisphere. So what does the right hemisphere do? As the chief researchers in this field have written, 'This "minor" hemisphere continues to perform as a very superior brain with a refined ability in stereognosis, and in pattern recognition and copying', yet there is no conscious sensation of these activities. And again: 'It is remarkable to see the superior stereognostic performance programmed by the minor hemisphere ... all unbeknown to the subject who sees it with amazement and chagrin.'[9] It is a case of the individual literally not knowing what his 'right brain' is doing.

As a general rule, then, the right half of the brain has a major role to play in the field of visual activity and perception. When individuals with surgically altered brains are presented with a picture made up of two different halves, questions requiring verbal answers are programmed by the left hemisphere (which indicates recognition of that portion of the picture in the right half visual field). Problems requiring visual recognition are programmed by the right hemisphere (which indicates recognition of the half of the picture in the left half visual field). Other observations such as these have led research workers to conclude that the right hemisphere has non-linguistic, non-mathematical functions. 'Largely they involve the apprehension and processing of spatial patterns, relations and transformations. They seem to be holistic and unitary rather than analytic and fragmentary, and orientational more than focal, and to involve concrete perceptual insight rather than abstract, symbolic, sequential reasoning.'[10] In other words, mental imagery and visual perception is closely associated with the right hemisphere. It is a fact that psychic work depends to a large extent on a process of visualization, that is, creating mental imagery, so we are justified in associating the creative forces of the right, non-reasoning, non-verbal hemisphere with the alpha state and psychic techniques. We have observed that consciousness is a function of the left hemisphere, which is also responsible for analysis and reasoning. Now, these properties of brain are closely associated with the production of beta waves. In other words, we have a conflict of interest, as it were: psychic work depends upon the right hemisphere, but conscious control of visualization must be a function of the left hemisphere. The exercises described below are designed to overcome the conflict.

They should: (a) stimulate the creative right hemisphere of the brain, a part which is overwhelmed by the reasoning left hemisphere in most of us, and (b) reduce left hemisphere activity to the minimum possible, so that the activity of the right hemisphere can be guided but not overwhelmed. Together these two activities make up 'controlled awareness', 'relaxed attentiveness'; in other words, the alpha state, in which psychic events are possible.

Later in this book, I shall refer to the greater effectiveness of psychic work as one goes 'deeper' into the alpha state. This refers to the amplitude of the alpha waves which one's brain is producing. The greater the amplitude, the deeper the alpha state, and the more effective the psychic work. For readers who are struggling, the following analogy may be helpful. Waves wash up the beach six times a minute, let us say, but the size – or amplitude – of those waves is not constant. Some are larger than others. It is exactly the same with the electrical activity of the brain.

Of the two elements in the exercises described below (relaxation and visualization), relaxation is the easier to understand. You will no doubt recall that psychic work depends upon the transmission of psychic information from the subconscious to the conscious mind. This happens most effectively when the conscious mind is free from tension and not very active. Surprising as it may seem, this state can be brought about by physical relaxation. Physical and mental tension go together to a surprising degree: you have only to make an effort to relax your body next time you feel angry or upset to see how true this is. So, complete relaxation, or later simply breathing in and out five times, acts as a clearing process to quieten the activity of the conscious mind before psychic work.

But what of visualization? It should now be clear to you that psychic work depends upon the alpha state, and that the development of alpha is aided by the process of visualization. Now, it just so happens that no matter which psychic system you examine, visualization also forms a major part of the psychic techniques themselves. (We have already seen how PK effects can be induced by visualization in Chapter 2.) So by learning to visualize, you will simultaneously develop the ability to generate alpha and to function psychically. As we shall see, however, there are other ways of working psychically besides visualization. You can actually learn a 'trigger' technique which will switch on alpha at moments during the day when you wish to be psychic, but do not have time to go through the complete exercise. This is all explained later. We begin by learning to relax and visualize.

How to Develop Your Psychic Ability

So, how much effort is involved? We have found that practising the exercises described below for two fifteen-minute periods twice a day for about two to four weeks is enough to give you the ability to develop the correct frame of mind for psychic work whenever you want. You will also learn the trigger technique which is useful for psychic work at odd moments during the day. People sometimes ask whether it is possible to be psychic without using the full relaxation and visualization exercise. It is an interesting question, which needs careful consideration.

To start with, as I have already explained, ten per cent of the population are natural psychics. Such people may not want to spend much time with the basic psychic techniques, but may wish to move straight on to try the telepathic techniques in Chapter 4 and, indeed, all the other psychic techniques in this book. At this point I can almost hear readers asking if they can determine whether or not they are amongst this ten per cent. In fact it is comparatively easy to answer this question. There are two ways of doing so. First, you may wish to try – or refresh your memory about the results of – the PK test which I outlined at the end of Chapter 2. Most people find that their score increases significantly after they have used the relaxation and visualization exercise, if only once. But this would not necessarily be true for anyone who was a 'natural' psychic. So if there was very little difference between your results before and after trying the relaxation exercise, yet both these scores were significantly above chance, then you could assume you are a natural psychic. Second, you could try dowsing and divination. If you have outstanding success on your first attempts, once again this is reasonably strong evidence that you are naturally psychic. However, you should remember that both these techniques seem to work reasonably well for almost everybody whether or not they have spent much time on the exercises. This fact makes them . . .

An easy and simple introduction to psychic techniques

It seems, as I shall explain later, that one's mind 'automatically' goes to the correct level for psychic work while one is dowsing or using a divination system. Perhaps it is significant that both these techniques use tools to display the psychically received information. In any event, for those who cannot, will not or do not wish to try the following exercise, which really is very easy, I suggest a start with dowsing (Chapter 8) or divination (Chapter 11). These techniques often lead on to a further exploration of the psychic world. But the ability to dowse and forecast the future is extremely remarkable in itself! As a general rule, anyone who does not have the time or inclination to go through the following exercises should clear his or her mind by breathing deeply five times and relaxing as much as possible before trying any psychic work.

Learning to relax and visualize

Remember – this is the key to ESP, psychic healing, problem solving, and a whole lot more. The results are well worth the time and (little) effort involved. Choose times when you are free from pressures. Whenever you choose, you will need two periods of about fifteen minutes, one in the morning and one in the evening (but not when you have a full stomach). Here is what you will do.

1.   Sit down comfortably on a soft chair with your back vertical and well supported. Your thighs should be parallel to the floor with your knees slightly apart. The angle between the upper and lower parts of your legs at the knee should be as near ninety degrees as possible. Your feet should point forward, although they may be slightly apart. Although a headrest is not essential, as it is quite easy to balance the head in an upright position, if you do find that your head flops on one side when you relax then it may help. Overall, the idea is to find a position where the body muscles can completely relax and are free from any tension. To ensure that this is so, you will need to ensure that you are not wearing any tight clothing (remove a tie, for example, before you start). Some people try the exercise when lying down full length on a bed; there is no basic objection to this approach, but the association of bed, relaxation and sleep may make you fall asleep, which is of no help whatsoever!

2.   Close your eyes. The room should be a reasonable

temperature, not too stuffy, but certainly not too cold either. There should not be any distracting lights shining into your face when you try the exercise.

3.   Test the tension in your body by checking each area in turn. Roll your head from side to side and concentrate on the muscular tension. You will probably find that you become aware of tightness which you previously did not know about. Relax these muscles. Do the same for your face, shoulders, arms and legs by consciously 'feeling' them in your mind. You will probably be astonished at the tension you have built up, particularly if this is the first time you have tried it.

4.   Say to yourself mentally, 'I am very peaceful'. This may not be true, but you should not regard saying it as either self-deception or trying to force yourself into a peaceful frame of mind. Forcing yourself to be peaceful is a contradiction that could never work! If you are slightly tense, a way of helping yourself is to imagine vividly in your mind's eye a place where you feel you could be totally relaxed. Picture yourself, perhaps, lying full length on a sun-soaked beach with the waves breaking leisurely on the sand. Whatever image you use, the mental phrase is 'I am very peaceful'. (Do not be too upset if you find your mind wandering. When you realize what is happening, repeat three times: 'Not now. At this time, I am very peaceful.' After practising you should find that your mind will remain on your relaxation.)

5.   When you have quietened mental activity by a conscious thought of peace and quiet, you can begin to relax each part of your body in turn. The feeling associated with complete relaxation will be heaviness. This is caused by a complete loss of muscle tension. The way to achieve this effect is to imagine as vividly as possible that your dominant hand is heavy. Repeat mentally, 'My right (or left) hand is getting heavy'. (Sometimes right-handed people feel their left hand getting heavy when they do this, in which case they should transfer their attention to the left hand. It is not important.) You will find that it is easy to relax your muscles, because the weight of the hand appears to increase as the muscles relax, making it lie more heavily on the chair. The feeling of heaviness is quite unmistakable and very pleasant. Sometimes it is associated with heaviness in other parts of the body, perhaps the opposite arm. Whether this is so or not,

it will be very easy to generalize the feeling of heaviness to the remainder of the body. Imagine the heaviness spreading up that arm, across your chest and back, then down your other arm. It can then travel down your abdomen and legs. You should transfer your attention between each part of the body fairly slowly. Before you move on from one part to the next, mentally repeat: 'My forearm is getting heavy'; 'My upper arm is getting heavy'; 'My chest and back are getting heavy'; and so on, for each part of your body in turn.

6.   The final phase of relaxation is to ensure that your abdomen is relaxed. This is done by repeating mentally, 'Right in my middle, down there, is pleasantly warm.' You should be able to achieve complete relaxation of your body, and you are then ready to try alpha. This is done by visualization, which is a process of creating mental imagery with the mind. In other words, although you cannot actually see anything, you form a mental perception of a situation or object. Most people find it easy to create a vivid mental image or picture after only a little practice. It is this procedure which stimulates the production of alpha in the brain. The details of visualization are not cut and dried. For example, Silva teaches its students to imagine a mental screen onto which all their visualization is projected. The screen is imagined to be some distance away from the body. This is done while sitting upright with the eyes turned upwards (behind closed lids) at an angle of twenty degrees to the horizontal. (If you were lying down, the screen and body would take the same relative positions.) Other authorities on visualization, however, do not suggest the use of a mental screen: they claim that simply forming a vivid mental image or picture is sufficient. What is best for you is probably what you are most comfortable with.

7.   Once you are happy with your procedure for visualization, create the following images (eyes closed, remember):
    (a)   Any brightly coloured object such as an orange or lemon.
    The discovery of one particular colour which you can perceive most vividly is the goal. Basically, the exercise enables you to think creatively, a process with which we have very often lost touch these days. *Note:* if you find the first exercise easy, the others will be no problem. So ensure that you have achieved it before moving on. Avoid thinking

about what you are doing; the time to assess any experience is after you have finished.

(b)   Try to visualize yourself walking around the object. Touch it, feel it and look at the texture. The more vivid your imagery, the better. You will be able to use this procedure for solving problems and more practice now will aid you later on.

(c)   Visualize another person or a scene for which you feel some particular affinity. There will be some inner experiences and reactions. Try to remember these, but do not analyse them yet.

(d)   Count down from five to one. Each number might form the image of a solid object on your mental screen. Be satisfied that you have a genuine perception of a number before counting downwards. This can take anything from ten seconds to three minutes. Each time that you do count down breathe out deeply. (When you come to do this, you may find that your breathing has been regular and shallow. This is a sign of deep rest of the body.) Breathing deeply while you count down will do two things: first, it will send the body to a deeper state of rest, which is good because it is easier to lose awareness of the body when it is relaxed; second, it will set up an association between the five deep breaths and your brain activity, so that the five deep breaths come to act as a trigger which lowers your brain activity towards alpha levels. The most important thing is to keep your conscious mind active but controlled – this is the state of controlled awareness which we shall encounter many times in psychic work. Try going deeper by counting from fifty or one hundred to one. You may be able to feel the deepening of your state of mind. Practise visualization.

8.   After a time, when you are happy with your achievements, come back to normal levels of mind by using the following method. Repeat these phrases mentally: 'I will feel much, much better each time I go down to the alpha level and I will keep control of the images I create. I am now coming back up to normal levels of mind by counting from one to ten. As I do so, I will have no headache or feeling of discomfort of any kind. I want to open my eyes, and I will be able to open my eyes, wide bright and clear.' Count slowly from one to ten. Do not rush it! As you come back to a normal level of mind, notice how

awareness of your body gradually returns. If you are still deep by the count of five, gently move your arms. Flex them, clench the hands and stretch the arms upwards. Then breathe out deeply and enjoy the feelings of stretching each part of the body. When you reach ten, stand up slowly and open your eyes. You may find that it takes a little while to come back to normal awareness, so do not immediately jump off the chair and rush about. Take your time.

Using the exercise for psychic work
The enjoyable feelings of relaxation will help you to recover from the stresses of the day. However, the exercise does more than that. The gradual development of mental imagery is aided by the relaxation to the point where you function in alpha. You will know that you have achieved this when you can relax quickly and control your visualization. For most people, this takes about four weeks. And then you are ready to try psychic work! There are two ways you can do this:

1. By using two fifteen-minute periods of visualization each day to achieve some objective (healing, ESP, obtaining your goals and desires, problem solving, or indeed anything you wish to try). Full details of the methods of these techniques are included in the relevant chapters.
2. By using the five deep breaths to trigger an alpha state which you can use at any time of the day for ESP, dowsing, divination, PK and other techniques.

The effectiveness of the five deep breaths as a trigger depends upon its continued association with the alpha state. This requires that you go through the full relaxation and visualization exercise fairly regularly – at least once a day – even if you are not using it for healing or some other specific objective. If you do not have a special objective, simply go through the full exercise and mentally repeat statements like: 'I am relaxing completely and all stress and tension is going away completely.' At some point during this exercise, make sure you count down from five to one, breathing out each time you repeat a number.

If you are using the full exercise twice a day for some objective, the association is automatically reinforced as you count down and breathe out during the exercise. Of course, you can also incorporate statements like: 'I am relaxing completely and all stress and tension is going away.' You can do this for whatever you require: better sleep, better health, better relationships and so on. However, that is not the main theme of this book. Suffice it to say that statements like those have a very powerful effect in the alpha state. In the next chapter, we shall examine some of the practical ways of developing telepathic ability. However, at this point we should examine some specific queries about both the exercise described above and the alpha state.

(a) *If you cannot find time for the exercise* This is a question of motivation. If you really want to, you can find time during the day, even if you only manage it once. If it is impossible to do even once a day, use it in bed at night. Sometimes noise or other people can be distracting during the day, but you will always have time in bed at night. In this case, do not use one to ten to come out, but drift gently off to sleep by saying mentally, 'I have now finished visualization and I will have a sound restful night's sleep.'

(b) *If you cannot relax* Everyone can, but in the early stages there may be distractions such as itching, swallowing and so on. As you practise, these problems will disappear and if they trouble you early on, then you can gently scratch or swallow as necessary.

(c) *If you have trouble with visualization* Visualization is the key to the whole procedure. Usually it proceeds from discrepant images with little colour (indeed, you may not be sure you have an image) through moving imagery, of whatever form you wish, to controlled visualization of complete situations. Sometimes, however, it seems to be a random chain of thoughts which run through the mind, apparently out of control like an absent-minded dream. This is quite natural; in fact it is a kind of dreaming, but it is not the aim of these exercises. Although you would feel better after fifteen minutes of this idle, relaxed daydreaming, you are trying to visualize for your own benefit. Only practice will let you succeed.

(d) *Coming out again after the session or in an emergency* There is no danger of being 'stuck' in the alpha state. You might enjoy it so much that you do not want to come out, but that is not the same thing! Remember in any case that your aim is to develop alpha during the day, and live normally with it. If you were 'stuck' in alpha, you would feel more creative and calm, but this would hardly be a bad thing. However, if you do feel that this might worry you, do the exercise in bed at night. Afterwards drop off to sleep naturally.

(e) *Staying in alpha with your eyes open*   Many books claim that it is impossible to stay in alpha with your eyes open. This is quite wrong. For one thing, we have seen that ten per cent of the population spend a great deal of their time in alpha naturally. And secondly, scientific research has shown that people who practise Buddhism, TM, Silva, or visualization all develop prolonged alpha during the day. Of course it all takes time. But the results are worth while.

(f) *How do you feel when you are in alpha?*   You feel distinctly calmer and more peaceful. I remember the first thing I discovered was that I did not feel the need to react to people with aggression or hostility. Unpleasantness and difficulties seemed to wash over me instead of 'hooking' me and making me respond irrationally or irritably. This varies, of course, but everyone finds that they start getting on better with other people and interacting with them in a more friendly and productive way. And, obviously, the frequency of spontaneous psychic experiences will increase dramatically.

(g) *Working psychically with the eyes open*   Whether or not you can do this depends upon both you and the technique you are using. With some techniques – divination and dowsing, for example – you *have* to keep your eyes open. The key to success here is being in alpha and being able to direct your attention inwards while forming a suitable mental image or question directed towards what you wish to achieve. Other techniques – healing, for example – are best done with the eyes closed. More details can be found in the relevant chapters.

(h) *Working psychically without practising the visualization exercise*   Psychic work depends upon the alpha state. You learn to develop the alpha state by learning visualization. So the ability to use your psychic faculties can be increased by means of visualization. But this is not to suggest that every psychic technique depends on visualization. For example, divination with the *I Ching* is conducted while you think of the question you want answered. Dowsing may involve a mental image or a mental question. And you will find that an apparently idle thought crossing your mind while you are in alpha can lead to a telepathic contact.

I think that covers most of the points which people raise about the exercise and the alpha state. We must now turn our attention to putting what you have learnt into action.

REFERENCES AND NOTES

1   An account of this work can be found in L. Watson, *Supernature* (Hodder and Stoughton, London, 1973), pp. 255–6.

2   See, for example, Watson, op. cit., p. 140.

3   Watson, op. cit., p. 256.

4   W. James, *Varieties of Religious Experience* (Longmans Green and Company, London, 1929).

5   There are many similar reports of such effects. See, for example, G. Schmeidler and R. McConnell, *ESP and Personality* (Yale University Press, New Haven, Conn., 1958), and J.B. Rhine, *The Reach of the Mind* (Faber, London, 1948).

6   As a good general introduction to the subject, see P. Russell, *The TM Technique* (Routledge and Kegan Paul, London, 1976).

7   I have shortened, and therefore reworded slightly, this quotation. For more information about Silva, see J. Silva and P. Miele, *The Silva Mind Control Method* (Granada, London, 1980); or write to BCM Learning, London WC1N 3XX, or Silva Mind Control International, Inc., P.O. Box 1149, Laredo, TX 78040, USA.

8   All these experiments are described in K. Popper and J. Eccles, *The Self and Its Brain* (Springer International, 1977), chapters E5 and E6, p. 311 *et seq.*

9   Ibid., p. 316.

10 Ibid., chapters E5 and E6.

4.

Telepathy in Action

One very well known technique which frequently has astonishing results is that of sending messages to someone. What you are actually doing is attracting some other person's attention by placing a 'signal' in his or her mind. In telepathic exercises like these, there are certain conditions which give rise to a higher rate of success. Obviously you should be relaxed and quiet. This gives you control over the conditions at your end of the contact. You cannot, however, assume that the person you wish to contact is in a receptive frame of mind. If he is very occupied with an animated discussion or argument, the message which you plant in his subconscious is unlikely to be noticed by his conscious mind. Remember, telepathy is not a conversation between two minds. Rather, the sender is implanting a message in the subconscious of the receiver which he will only notice as an emotion or feeling. Thus, if you want someone to telephone you, he may indeed call after the mental signal has reached him, but he will not have done so because he knew you wanted him to ring. If you were to ask, you would probably be told: 'Oh, I just felt I had to ring you.' Equally, if you send a signal to a friend, asking him to bring a book for you to read, when he sees you he will say something like: 'I thought you might want this.' On the other hand, if you are transmitting an image to someone's mind, you may find that he has a mental flash of what you are sending. This will work best if both you and the receiver are at alpha; the results can then be really astounding – almost frightening.

Here is another telepathic technique. Next time you are in a situation where someone may be waiting to serve you – a waiter in a restaurant, say – take five deep breaths and visualize, as vividly as you can, the waiter turning round to look at you and walking across to your table. (You will probably find that it works better to start with if you close your eyes briefly.) Often when you do this, the waiter will indeed turn and look at you. After you have been doing this for a while, your strength and ability to attract attention increase, so even if you do not succeed at first, keep trying.

I would like to think that is all there is to telepathy, but alas, such is not the case. Some people cannot visualize with their eyes open, and others are slightly embarrassed at closing them in case they achieve their objective so quickly that the waiter, say, gets across to them before they are aware of it! Of course such feelings quite destroy any chance you have of succeeding. So here is a different technique. Still in the same restaurant, take five deep breaths and imagine a string between you and the waiter. Imagine a pulse of energy collecting at your forehead and then travelling along the string to strike the waiter's head. Dr Jean Burns gives a lovely description of what happens when someone receives a pulse. She describes an incident in a lecture room, when somebody had his hand up to ask a question, but the lecturer had not noticed. Dr Burns tried to help by sending a pulse to the lecturer to attract his attention. He jumped up into the air, spun a half circle and finished up looking straight at Dr Burns, who then pointed weakly to the man with the question![1] Such dramatic results do not always occur. It may be some time before either of these methods works consistently well, so you can aid the development of your skill by practising. If you have a friend who is willing to try, you could spend some time trying to send pulses to each other. It will function better if you are emotionally close to the person you work with, because you can then establish a good rapport. My experience suggests that the results will feel very pleasant. Whenever I have tried this, a deep feeling of peace has come over me and I have experienced a sensation of great calm. Very relaxing, yet difficult to describe. After a short time (say, two hours) you may well discover that the pulses become very clear and you are certain when one has been received because of a feeling you get in your mind – unique and very rewarding.

Either of those methods should eventually produce good results. Here is something else to try. Breathe deeply five times. Close your eyes while sitting comfortably in a chair with all the body supported, and visualize as clearly as possible a friend going to the telephone in his or her house, picking up the receiver and dialling your number. See every detail of the scene, in as bright and clear a picture as you can manage. Keep this up for at least ten minutes, and if your mind wanders, bring it back gently to the image. If you want to go to a deeper level of mind, count slowly down from ten to one and continue with the visualization. You may well be surprised when your friend rings you; do not be too downhearted if nothing happens, however – he may be out, or concentrating on some work of his own. Keep trying.

Perhaps you are wondering if there is any way in which you can develop telepathic abilities while going about everyday business. The answer is – yes, by becoming more sensitive to the information that your subconscious is presenting to you. Normally your conscious activity excludes just about every impression your subconscious throws at you, unless it is a very powerful one such as fear or anger or sickness. Since all telepathic information is received subconsciously, it must go through a filtering process before it reaches awareness. If you think about it for a minute, you will realize that not all the information received by our normal sense organs manages to reach our minds – a radio or television in the background is filtered out after a while because the brain realizes that it is of no importance. But if there was an announcement of a rail or air crash which could have involved one of your family, your attention is immediately switched back on to it. Clearly something was listening all the time, but the conscious mind was not aware of it. And I have already mentioned how one hears one's own name at a party amongst all the indistinguishable background noise. So by learning to be more responsive to, or aware of, the information coming from the subconscious, the chance of noticing information received psychically is greatly improved. Basically there are two ways of doing this. Here they are.

Learning to be aware of impressions
Sit quietly in a chair and let mental activity decrease as much as possible. Focus your attention on the weight of your body pressing onto the chair – can you feel the chair seat and back? Mentally examine each place where you feel your body touching the chair, and assess whether you usually notice these sensations when you are sitting down. Slowly shift your attention to the feeling of the clothes resting loosely on your skin. Can you distinguish between cotton and wool or man-made fibre? See if you can pick out the pattern on the surface of the material. Now

try and feel any movement of air across the skin; perhaps it is moving the hairs on your arms and legs. Does one side of your face feel warmer than the other, and is this accompanied by brighter light from one side or the other? Finally bring into your picture the sensations in your feet and legs – how do your clothes touch your body? What are the sensations in your feet where they touch the ground? If you have been able to focus clearly on each of these feelings, try to assimilate them so that you are aware of all of them at the same time. Hold your impressions for two or three minutes.

Once you have become adept at this exercise (and you will be surprised how quickly your skill develops if you practise two or three times a day), it is helpful to develop your awareness still further by concentrating on the sensations being received by your other senses – what can you smell, taste and hear? Probably there are all sorts of noises in the background which are unfamiliar to you. Try to identify them by listening carefully; at the same time see if you can keep awareness of all the impressions you noticed in the first half of the exercise. Most people find it very difficult to keep awareness at such a high level. If you do not succeed, do not be concerned. The very act of trying will enable you to listen more carefully to impressions from the subconscious.

A variation of the technique above relates to emotions and feelings. I sometimes find myself noticing a tenseness, irritation or uneasiness growing in certain situations. Next time this happens to you, do not ignore it or avoid it by frantically throwing your attention into some other activity. Stop what you are doing and analyse the way you feel. See whether the sensation is located in one part of your body. Examine your attitude and try to place the emotion you feel – is it jealousy, fear, anger, sadness or what? Be especially careful to examine whether the emotion is directed against yourself or somebody else. You can also try an exercise in awareness when you are having a conversation. See if you can identify the emotions and feelings, thoughts and impressions that cross your mind. These are what always make up those familiar feelings: 'I disliked him from the moment I met him' or 'It was love at first sight'.

By trying these simple self-awareness exercises, you will increase your awareness of parts of your mind normally inaccessible to you; in fact you will come to realize how little of your mind is used consciously. One example which illustrates the point should be familiar to many readers. When I took my young children out into the country to look at a waterfall, they quickly became bored despite the glorious sunshine, the reflections on the water, the rainbows produced in the spray, and all the other sights and sounds. While we adults were looking and listening, finding our attention fully occupied, the children were saying, 'Daddy, can we go and play? There's nothing to do here.' This was because their awareness is only advanced in matters which directly concern them – while adult awareness tends to be high when the self is not involved. Think back to the last time you were unjustly reprimanded by your superior at work. I would imagine all you were aware of was a blank mind with a feeling of outrage and anger. At such an emotional moment, you were almost certainly unaware of other thoughts and feelings in your mind: your attention was directed totally towards your own feelings of anger or outrage. In fact a system has been proposed for the classification of areas in which self-awareness is lacking: these are called inclusion, control and affection areas.[2]

Inclusion areas of life are basically those in which there is the possibility of being accepted (or rejected) by a group. You would be classed as having a lack of self-awareness in inclusion situations if you could not face a group of people because of shyness. The shyness is actually based on a fear of rejection by other people, but you are unaware of this. All you will experience is the feeling of trepidation at the thought of meeting new people. Another example is the person who talks too much – he is doing this because of a subconscious fear that people may not find him interesting. Although he is aware of himself talking, he does not know why he is saying so much, nor is he aware of how people around him are responding. Once again, his awareness is limited to only one part of the feelings in his mind.

Control areas are concerned with life situations where leadership is called for. Most people work below somebody and above others; but a person who lacks self-awareness in this field of life may want to lead all the time. He may be a domineering type, always aggressively putting forward his own plans and adopting a commanding attitude. Other people may have the opposite problem – they wish to be led, and are unable to control their lives. Often a person like this will feel a complete failure when he makes an ordinary mistake. He lacks awareness of how he creates problems for himself and is unable to go back to a problem and start again.

The third area is affection. Many people have difficulty expressing their feelings for other people, or coming to terms with the fact that not everybody is going to like them. Often people do not realize that they are preventing themselves getting close to others because they fear rejection. Someone who lacks self-awareness in this area of life may behave offensively or excessively amiably. In neither case does he really allow people to come close to him, because he cannot handle a fear of rejection after affection has been shown. What is most upsetting is that he does not even realize how he is behaving, let alone why, and often wonders why he is lonely.

You will find that a few minutes' analysis of the day before you go to sleep can be very revealing. You can come to realize why you feel as you do in these situations, and after a time you will find that an awareness of your feelings will aid your relationships with others. However, as far as psychic work is concerned, cultivation of awareness is important because you will come to notice and identify the impressions which your subconscious mind presents to you much more easily.

Listening to your subconscious

The section on consciousness has probably helped you to see the functions of the subconscious mind more easily. To recap, it is the part of the brain which works constantly, even when we are asleep, by controlling breathing, heart rate, gut movements and so on. (Breathing and other subconscious functions can be controlled consciously as well, of course; but when you are asleep, the subconscious has complete control of your body.) Additionally, it processes information and acts as a filter for the conscious mind. Sometimes you will have been trying to remember a name or place, but been quite unable to recall it. Doubtless it has popped into your consciousness quite unexpectedly later on, after it was needed. This is because the subconscious has been working through the memory to find what you require. Also, it is why you often choose to 'sleep on a problem' − by the time you wake up, the subconscious has a neatly prepared answer ready. I have mentioned that all psychic information is received in the subconscious and there is the danger that you might not notice if it were to be presented to the conscious mind. Here is an example of this effect. I keep my car keys on a ring which also holds keys for my parents' and brother's cars. They all look similar, so I mark my own with white paint. However, this is no use at night and I end up trying all the keys until I come to the correct door key for my own car. After I started the exercises described in this chapter, a remarkable thing began to happen. At first I was unaware of it, but after some time, I stopped to focus on the new sensation that I felt each time I unlocked the door. I realized that I was getting a quite unexpected and vivid flash in my mind, in the form of a thought – 'Not that one' – each time I picked up the wrong key. This was always right until I started consciously thinking: 'This is the wrong one.' Obviously this kind of conscious thought does not relate in any way to information received physically. After I made an effort to stop the thoughts, the 'flashes' came back – and they are still 100 per cent correct. I wonder how much 'inspiration' is the product of one's own mind, and how much is psychically received from other individuals?

If you make an effort to listen to your subconscious you should be able to repeat this experience. One way is to listen out for strong signals from the subconscious. If a thought flashes into your mind unexpectedly, don't ignore it; follow it up and see if it is of any use and, if possible, whether it is accurate or not. Then ask yourself a mental question related to that subject. The answer will be the first thing that comes into your mind, although it may not be as clear as you hope. This once happened to a colleague of mine. He had been told that his father was in hospital, and had travelled straight to the hospital from work, without knowing what the problem was. When he arrived, he met the doctor, introduced himself and asked, 'What is the problem?' As he later told me, before the doctor spoke, he had a clear impression of somebody stuck in a doorway, shouting 'Shut the door' as it shook violently on its hinges. I can imagine how he felt when the doctor told him that his father had a valve in his heart that was not closing properly. This type of experience is much more common than generally realized, and so you should make an effort to notice all the subconscious impressions which break through to your awareness.

In the next chapter, we shall explore more ways that you can develop ESP, particularly through dream analysis. Since the conscious mind is less active during sleep, this provides a way in which everybody can get in touch with their 'psychic power'.

REFERENCES AND NOTES

1 Jean Burns, *Your Innate Psychic Powers* (Sphere, London, 1981), p. 23.
2 W.C. Schutz, *Here Comes Everybody*.
   The subject is also discussed in Burns, op. cit., pp. 198–203.
   Note: there are many books which provide practical exercises for the development of psychic ability. See, for example, Burns, op. cit.; Sophia Williams *You Are Psychic*; H. Carrington, *Your Psychic Powers and How to Develop Them* (Aquarian Press, Wellingborough, 1976).

5.

The Psychic Power of Dreams

A major survey was conducted in 1890 by the British Society for Psychical Research.[1] It was designed to investigate the possibility of psychic communication in dreams, and involved the study of more than 20,000 responses from different parts of the world. One example is typical of the many cases recorded which seemed to show telepathy acting in dreams. Canon Warburton, a member of the society, was staying with his brother in London for a few days. He arrived home one evening to find a note from his brother, stating that he had gone to a dance and would be back around 1 a.m. Canon Warburton decided to wait up in a chair by the fire, but he soon fell asleep. He woke up sharply at one o'clock when a vivid dream passed through his mind. As he reported later, he 'saw' his brother coming out of a drawing room at the head of a flight of stairs, tripping, and falling down the steps. When his brother arrived home at half-past one, the first words he spoke were: 'I have just had the narrowest escape from a broken neck, when I caught my foot coming out of the ballroom.' The similarity between the two descriptions is astonishing. It is as if Canon Warburton had been watching when his brother slipped. This was probably telepathy, but there are also many cases on record of precognitive and clairvoyant dreams. In another chapter, we have seen how Abraham Lincoln dreamed of his own assassination days before it took place. To emphasize how important such dreams can be, let us look at some more examples. Later, we will study the techniques which can be used to obtain these dreams.

In 1966, the Welsh village of Aberfan suffered a horrifying tragedy. The coal tips above the village had been loosened by three days of continuous rain, and on the morning of 21 October, their foundations gave way. Millions of tons of slag and coal slipped onto the village, killing 144 people – of whom 128 were schoolchildren. One of these schoolchildren had apparently foreseen the disaster in a dream, because two weeks before the calamity she said to her mother, 'Mummy, I am not afraid to die.' Then, the day before the landslip, she spoke of a dream in which she had seen the school engulfed by 'something black'. She was buried in a communal grave with the other children.

After he had heard about this, a consultant psychiatrist at a local hospital decided to investigate precognition of the disaster. By means of a newspaper appeal, he asked people who believed that they had had dreams about the event before it happened to contact him. One startlingly accurate account was delivered by a forty-seven year old woman from Plymouth who claimed that she had had a dream which had predicted the tragedy. This was confirmed by the fact that she spoke about her dream *the day before the tragedy* in front of six witnesses at a church meeting. This was the way she described it: 'I saw an old school house in a valley, a Welsh miner and an avalanche of coal hurtling down a mountain.' She went on to describe a rescuer and a small boy who was saved, both of whom were later recognized at the scene of the rescue operation.[2]

Some scientific investigations have been conducted on this subject, and seem to provide good evidence for the reality of psychic dreams.[3] At the Maimonides Medical Centre in New York Dr Montague Ullman has set up a Dream Laboratory. His procedure for investigating telepathy in dreams is based on waking up a subject immediately after a dream, so that he can remember its contents. (As long ago as 1950, scientists had identified the rapid eye movements (REM) that occur only while a sleeping person is dreaming. REM makes it very easy to check when a person is having a dream – you simply watch his eyes while he sleeps.) Dr Ullman signalled to an 'agent' when his subject was dreaming, and the agent then tried to influence the dreams of the subject. Not all the results were significant, but the correct hits are so striking that they leave no room for doubt. On one occasion, the subject was a Dr Erwin and the agent was a member of the laboratory staff, Miss Joyce Plosky. She selected a picture of Salvador Dali's *The Sacrament of the Last Supper*, which shows Christ with his disciples against a background of a fishing boat on the sea. She then tried to transmit this to Dr Erwin. After his dream had finished, he was awoken and recounted what he had experienced: 'An ocean, strangely beautiful with fishing boats. A dozen or so men pulling a fishing boat ashore. The Mediterranean area, perhaps Biblical times. I think of Christmas, feeding the multitude with fish and loaves.'

The Dream Laboratory extended their work to test for precognition in dreams by asking the subject to dream about an experience which the laboratory staff *would create for him next day*. Malcolm Bessent, one particularly good subject, managed to dream correctly about the event which was later to be staged for him on eight consecutive tests! But despite this good evidence for the precognitive potential of dreams, it is probably the anecdotal accounts which convince most people: for example, the Aberfan episode and Lincoln's dream of his assassination.

It is reasonable to assume that both telepathy and precognition occur in dreams fairly frequently, but that we cannot remember when it happens, simply because of the difficulty of recalling our dreams when we wake up in the morning. However, this problem is easily overcome: there is a fairly simple procedure for recalling dreams immediately after they have occurred. For example, suppose that you wished to be warned of any dangers you might run into on a car journey. You would spend some time just before you fell asleep programming yourself to receive information about any dangers that you face. To do this, you need to learn the relaxation exercise described in Chapter 3, and use it just before you fall asleep. When you are relaxed, visualize yourself writing down the dream with a pencil and paper placed by the bed. Mentally repeat: 'I want to have a dream which contains information about my journey and any dangers I face. I will wake up with a dream in mind, and remember it so I can write it down.' You will probably find that you wake up during the night with a vivid dream. Write it down at once. Do the same immediately you wake up in the morning – any conscious thoughts will take it clean out of your mind. Whatever dream you can remember should contain the information you require. Here is an example of the sort of results that can be obtained with this technique.

While I was writing this, I decided to travel to London to do some research. Unfortunately, the weather was atrocious. Blizzards had reduced traffic flow to a crawl and blocked many roads. The night before I was due to leave, I went through the relaxation exercises and mentally programmed myself to receive information about the best route to take; the one that would get me there safely and quickly, in fact. During the night, I woke up with a vivid image of children skating on thin ice and one falling through into the water. This did not seem to have much significance, but I knew better than to dismiss the dream. I set out down the M6 motorway, which is normally the fastest route. About thirty miles from the start of the journey, there was a traffic bulletin on the radio which warned of black ice on, amongst other roads, the M6. After a time, these dreams happen so reliably that there can be no question of doubting them. This is now my attitude, so I did not hesitate to leave the motorway as soon as possible.

My journey continued on an alternative route and took much longer than I had planned, although I did arrive safely. Not until I phoned home the next day did I know that on the section of motorway I had been planning to use there was a thirty-vehicle pile-up caused by a lorry skidding on black ice. Thus you cannot always be sure of how the psychic information will be presented, but there will be enough clues to let you figure it out. The important point is that you probably will not receive a warning in a clearly phrased instruction ('Don't travel on the M6'). The nature of the brain and mind dictates that there must be a symbolic, visual representation of the answer to your question.

From time to time, there have been reports that people have obtained information in dreams which has led to financial gain or other material benefits. A typical example was related by José Silva, the founder of the Silva Mind Control courses mentioned in Chapter 3. When he was developing his mind control course, he was desperately short of money and almost gave up in despair. However, one night he had a dream in which three numbers appeared to him as though they were illuminated by a bright light. Thinking nothing of it at the time, he dismissed the dream. Next day, his wife asked him to visit a small town just across the Texas/Mexico border. He went with a friend and on the way told him about the dream. Now, here is the fascinating part of the story. When they visited a small shop in Mexico his friend pointed out a Mexican national lottery ticket – that had exactly the numbers seen by Silva in his dream. What would you have done? Silva bought the ticket there and then. It is almost unnecessary to add that he won a large prize![4]

Now, this was an unexpected dream which clearly involved clairvoyance and precognition. But the important point is that a psychic communication brought Silva some good fortune. I intend to leave it up to the reader to determine whether his own psychic faculty can do the same for him! A slightly different technique is available for solving problems by using the relaxation and visualization exercises. In the examples described below, the solution to a problem which had been bothering the person in question came quite unexpectedly in the form of mental images while he was half-asleep.

Kekulé was a nineteenth-century chemist who discovered the shape of the benzine molecule, a carbon/hydrogen compound which had confounded all previous attempts to describe its shape. As Kekulé dozed in front of his fire, an image of a snake with its tail in its mouth flashed across his mind. Suddenly he realized that this was the answer! The whole basis of organic ring chemistry was born in one flash when Kekulé realized that the molecule folded back on itself. Many similar examples have been recorded. Elias Howe, who developed the sewing machine, tried for months to design a method of stitching cloth with the up-and-down movement of a needle. All his efforts seemed to be in vain until he had a dream about native savages in the jungle. They were threatening him with their spears; at the tip of each spear was a hole with a thread hanging from it. This was true inspiration – the machine could be made to work perfectly by putting the cotton through the tip of the needle instead of the normal end.

It is not just mechanical inventions that have resulted from mental imagery. Many great works of music and poetry have been created in dream-like states of mind. For example, while dozing in a carriage, Mozart once found that an entire composition had come into his mind, and Coleridge created much of his poetry in a semi-conscious state. The phenomenon is well defined by scientists, who call it *hypnagogic imagery*. One laboratory which has specialized in investigating hypnagogic imagery is the Menninger Clinic, Topeka, Kansas. The director (Dr Elmer Green) and his staff have found that anyone who experiences hypnagogic imagery shows alpha or theta waves in their brain. (You should not be surprised to learn that imagery is associated with alpha waves.[5] As a function of the creative right brain hemisphere, this is exactly what one would expect.) To be fully aware of images produced as solutions to problems, the subject must remain conscious at the alpha level. Let me state at once that there is no clear answer as to whether or not hypnagogic imagery is psychic. The dividing line between psychic and non-psychic brain power is blurred, and the only suggestion I can make is that it is not important – if you can use the technique for solving problems, then it has a place in this book with ESP, dowsing, divination and so on.

The procedure is simple – during time in alpha, you mentally ask whatever question is troubling you, and hopefully your mind will create images that provide an answer. If you are ill, you might receive an image of the deficient organ in response to the question: 'What part of my body has a problem?' Alternatively, you could use the technique for helping yourself work out problems with your relationships, career or, indeed, just about anything you care to try.

The whole world of your subconscious is waiting to be tapped, and it has far more knowledge and power available than you realize. My advice is to learn the relaxation and visualization technique described in Chapter 3 and try it for yourself. You may find that your creativity and intuition increase dramatically, along with the more obvious benefits of developing your psychic dream and problem solving power.

REFERENCES AND NOTES

1   Reported in Thelma Moss, *The Probability of the Impossible* (Routledge and Kegan Paul, London, 1976), pp. 170-71.

2   J.C. Barker, 'Premonitions of the Aberfan disaster', *Journal of the Society for Psychical Research,* vol. 44, 1967, pp. 170-80.

3   For an account of this work, see M. Ullman, S. Krippner, A. Vaughan, *Dream Telepathy* (Turnstone Press, Wellingborough, 1973).

4   J. Silva and P. Miele, *The Silva Mind Control Method* (Granada, London, 1980). pp. 49-51.

5   This subject is discussed in a paper by I. Oswald, 'Visual Imagery and Alpha Waves', *Quarterly Journal of Experimental Psychology,* vol. 9, 1957, pp. 113-18.

6.

More Exercises in Telepathy, Clairvoyance and Precognition

A distant viewing experiment

These tests are well worth carrying out even though they involve considerable planning. The aim is to receive information about a distant location from the minds of people who are there. The interpretation of the results is entirely subjective, but if you do find similarities between the target and responses, they will probably be quite striking. The experimental protocol is set out below in a step-by-step sequence, with explanatory notes at each stage.

The experiment can be done with only two people, although there is no limit to how many can take part. If you have some independent observers, your results will be less subject to personal bias. This applies particularly to the interpretation of the results. The subjects who are going to receive the information from the transmitters should have no way of contacting the transmitters until all the tests are finished. Thus, if you are trying this with a friend, ask him to 'send' a mental image of his location at a particular time on a certain day. At that time, you should record any impressions that come into your mind and attempt a drawing if possible. This will later act as a comparison with a photograph or description of the site that the transmitter should provide. When more than two people are involved (and an ideal number is four) the procedure will be as follows:

1.   Split into two pairs. One pair will consist of the receiver and his observer; the other is the transmitter and his observer.

2.   Before you begin, agree not to meet or discuss any aspect of the experiment until you have finished. The transmitter and his observer will drive out to a location selected by the observer after they have got into the car and started driving. They should

arrive at a pre-arranged time. The transmitter will concentrate on the location in whatever way he feels would help the receiver to obtain an image. Most people find that relaxing and simply viewing the scene works reasonably well. More advanced students will relax, go into alpha and visualize the receiver drawing the scene while they are actually looking at it. There is the opportunity for experiment, so try several techniques of sending the image.

3.   At the pre-arranged time, the receiver will relax and close his eyes. He records into a tape recorder whatever crosses his mind; always the very first thought without any analysis of it, no matter how silly it may sound. He may then attempt to draw any image he receives. People who have learnt to go down to alpha will find they have a higher success rate, particularly if the transmitter is also at alpha.

4.   After the pre-arranged transmitting time is over, the four should meet up again to discuss the results. There is always the danger that you can read into these experiments more than is actually there, so be as objective as possible. If you've got a 'hit', fantastic! Try again with the added sophistication of the technique described below. If not, wait until you are fresh (which probably means another day) and try again.

5.   After there has been a successful 'hit', you will need to let your elation die down. Then try it again, in a way that eliminates coincidence: without telling anyone else, the observer accompanying the transmitter should select twenty locations before the experiment begins. These will be placed in sealed envelopes and handed to a fifth person who drives the car. He selects an envelope at random when the team are setting out, and so introduces a randomizing effect into the experiment. If the receiver identifies the scene correctly, it is reasonable to suppose that he has not done so by chance alone. Note that the observers are present to stop any cheating. They must prevent contact between the transmitter and receiver, and ensure that the location really is unknown before the experiment starts. They may also act as judges of the results.

One result of consistently trying all these exercises is that you develop the ability to contact other people's minds as and when you choose. Obviously the ability to do this (or to obtain information to solve problems or protect oneself from possible harm) is very useful. But there is another reason to practise these simple exercises. Only by practising with telepathic, clairvoyant and precognitive techniques will your ability to visualize improve. And it is essential that you have the ability to visualize at alpha if you wish to use the techniques described in later chapters of this book.

An experiment in contact telepathy

By becoming more aware of information from the normal senses, you can increase your awareness of psychic impressions. One exercise which may be useful in developing psychic ability is *contact telepathy*. You initially receive information from the sense of touch, but soon begin to have flashes which can only be psychic. The technique is taken from *Psychic and Other ESP Party Games* by David Hoy.[1]

Ask somebody to hide a small object while you are out of the room. Before you re-enter, put on a blindfold so that you cannot see anything. When you return, take the wrist of the person who has hidden the object gently between the tips of your forefinger and thumb. If you walk slowly across the room, you soon discover that your guide is making subconscious movements towards the object. If you move away from it, he increases his resistance and you feel a tug on your wrist. If you approach it, his resistance lessens. So by appearing to guide him round the room, you obtain information about the object from his movements. Very simple and not exactly psychic! But sooner or later, flashes of intuition about the location of the object come into your mind unbidden. The longer the period of practice, the better the results. Clearly, by using the physical senses, you have improved the receptivity of your conscious mind to psychic information. Probably this is by telepathy, reading the mind of the person who has hidden the object.

Card guessing experiments in ESP

If you wish to use the type of card that Rhine worked with (the Zener cards), they can be obtained from the Society for Psychical Research, 1 Adam and Eve Mews, Kensington, London W8. They consist of packs of twenty-five cards of five designs. Alternatively, you can make your own Zener cards, using whatever designs you are happy with. Typical examples might be: a circle, a cross, a triangle, a star and a series of wavy lines. If you want to use ordinary playing cards, you can try and identify either the colour or the suit of each card. But no matter what cards you use, it is essential to analyse your results and compare them with the score expected by chance alone. For example, suppose you identify the colour of ordinary playing cards correctly sixty times out of one hundred in a test of clairvoyance. Is that score really indicative of clairvoyance, or can it be attributed to chance alone? The statistical analysis explained in the Appendix shows odds of 20 to 1 against this score having been the result of chance alone. This is not sufficiently strong evidence for you to be certain that clairvoyance has been demonstrated. You should really ignore any result unless the odds against having obtained it by chance are greater than 100 to 1. But if you consistently score at that level or higher, you can assume you are a pretty good psychic.

A test for clairvoyance

This is the easiest test to try. With ordinary playing cards, try to guess the colour or suit; with Zener cards, the design on the face. (It may be preferable to start with the either/or test of red and black playing cards because it is easier to analyse the results.) But in either case, you need at least two hundred guesses for the test to be worth while. Each pack used must be well shuffled between runs, so that you do not learn the sequence of cards in the pack.

Here is the method. Ask someone to shuffle the pack and place it face downwards on a table between himself and you. He will turn over the cards one at a time; but before he turns each card, you will write down your guess about it. After you have done this, your assistant writes down what it actually was, so that you can tot up your score afterwards and calculate the significance of your results. Do be sure, however, that you cannot see the cards which the dealer is turning over. Before you start, relax by breathing deeply five times, and ask your dealer to do the same. Remember that an interest in the experiment is essential, and that performance in such tests usually decreases as boredom increases. If you think that there is a danger of telepathic interference from the dealer, you could do this alone, but be sure that you do not cheat by marking down your guess *after* turning the card! In this case, you should write down your guess and then turn the card to see if you were correct. Mark your guess with a tick or cross, or if you are using Zener cards, write down what the design actually was. The first or most powerful impression in your mind is the most important one.

The first time I tried this test I had no success at all for some time. Then I discovered that by: (a) avoiding conscious thought, (b) lifting the card to my forehead, and (c) noticing the first impression in my mind, I could make my score increase dramatically. Later, an experienced psychic told me that one sometimes obtains 'interference' from cards on each side of the one you are trying to identify (this is discussed in the next chapter). This effect can be avoided by imagining the face of each card being scraped clean just before you make your guess. Another refinement in all such experiments is to use short runs of about ten guesses with pauses of fifteen or twenty seconds in between. This method tends to give a much higher success rate than a continual run from beginning to end.

Children make good subjects for these experiments. Conveniently, they can be bribed with sweets – a pack of five colours can be used to good effect. To test for clairvoyance, pick out one sweet at a time from the bag while it is behind your back. Ask the child what colour it is, and allow him to keep it if he is correct. (Be sure that he cannot see it before telling you the colour!) You can analyse these results in exactly the same way as the card-guessing scores.

A test for telepathy

These tests are less reliable than the ones for clairvoyance, because you are trying to guess the 'contents' of someone else's mind. However, if you wish to try, here is the method. Ask a friend to think of a card while you try and guess what it is. Write down your guess. Then ask him to write down what he was thinking of, so that you can mark your results later. Remember to break the experimental run into several short periods. Analyse your results using the Appendix.

A test for precognition

This test is perhaps the most interesting of all. You write down your guesses about the order in which a pack of cards will be dealt – but you do this *before* it has been shuffled or dealt out. This may sound extraordinary, but that is what precognition is all about.

In all these experiments, it is very important that you do not pick up any visual clues about the cards. Perhaps the best way of ensuring that this does not happen is to work with your back to the person who is dealing them. An independent observer to check for cheating might be useful, too. Of course, this also applies if you are working alone.

As an example of the results that can be obtained with such tests, while I was writing this I conducted a quick test of clairvoyance with ordinary playing cards. I guessed whether each one was red or black before turning it over; I had someone else shuffle the pack as well as possible before each of six runs through the pack. My score was 184 correct out of 312 guesses. Reference to the Appendix shows that this score would arise by chance only once in every 500 or more tests, each consisting of 312 guesses. To put it another way, the probability of there being no significance to these results is 0.2 per cent or 1 in 500. Reasonable evidence, I think, of clairvoyance.

REFERENCES

1.   D. Hoy, *Psychic and Other ESP Party Games*.

7.

Psychometry:
An Advanced Form of ESP

Psychometry is a special form of ESP. It is a technique which enables one to receive psychically information about an object simply by touching it. To illustrate this point, let us compare an analysis of an object with the five ordinary senses and a psychometric analysis. Suppose that you were given a piece of jewellery to examine. Normally, you would look at it from all angles, feel its weight and judge its age, value and other characteristics. This information would enable you to make certain deductions about its owner: man or woman, age, personal tastes and, perhaps, degree of affluence. You might in this way be able to build up quite a comprehensive picture of the object and its owner. Now, as we know, the psychic sense receives impressions through a mechanism which does not involve the usual sense organs. In telepathy, for example, the recipient or receiver will often close his eyes while he tries to receive impressions of any telepathic communication. In all cases of psychic work, too, the conscious mind is less active, and its analysis of sensory input is greatly reduced. Psychometry is a technique which involves all these characteristics; usually, one gently fingers an object, or holds it up to one's forehead, while passively noting any impressions which come to mind. The main problem in conducting a psychometric reading of an object is that one has somehow to be aware of the object under analysis, without consciously distorting the psychic impressions that are being received: primary process distortion is as much a problem with psychometry as with any other psychic technique. When we move on to examine the ways in which a psychometric ability can be developed, you will see that the exercises are designed to help you to develop further the art of 'controlled awareness': that is, the state in which conscious activity is reduced but full awareness is maintained. But let us first consider the mechanisms by which psychometry actually works.

It is possible that some cases of so-called psychometry are nothing more than examples of telepathic transmission of information between two individuals. After all, if someone offers an object for psychometric analysis, he probably knows a great deal about that object. Quite frequently, however, that explanation can be ruled out immediately, because the information obtained by the psychometrist just does not exist within the mind of any living person. An alternative explanation for the technique is that psychometry is 'merely' a direct form of clairvoyance. Some people – those who are trained or naturally psychic – might have the ability to concentrate their clairvoyant faculty on an object and 'extract' information about it in the same way that they would in a normal clairvoyance test. And indeed, because psychometry and clairvoyance are so similar, we may assume that they are different aspects of the same psychic technique.

We can now concentrate upon the methods and procedures which enable anyone to develop and practise psychometry with a fair degree of success. The key to success lies in the fact that psychometry is a receptive procedure, and not an 'expressed' or 'directive' power like healing or visualization. Much of the information received during a psychometric reading comes into the mind as a block and has to be sorted and delivered to consciousness without primary process distortion. However, many objects have a long history, perhaps involving several owners. This in itself can confuse the psychometrist, but the situation is made worse by the fact that it is not unknown for a psychometrist to receive precognitive information as well as historical or current information about an object. Because of this, training must centre upon two points: first, actually developing the ability to pick up information, and second, developing the ability to present that information coherently and accurately.

W.E. Butler has described the skills which are necessary to achieve those two abilities.[1] The first skill could be called 'observation without emotion or prejudice.' In the words of W.E. Butler, 'Most of us, because of psychological blind spots, tend to observe some things and fail to observe others, or else we confuse the sequence in which things took place.' This applies equally to information received through using the ordinary and psychic senses. Butler has suggested that observation is largely dependent upon directed attention. Therefore, exercises which develop this skill will produce a mind which can identify and sort out psychic impressions received during psychometry. (Of course, they will also improve the ability to register psychic impressions received during any other psychic technique.) The first such exercise is called 'Kim's Game'. It involves having an assistant place about twenty small objects such as screws, buttons and rings on a tray. You then direct your attention on to the objects, for a couple of minutes only, after which you cover the tray with a cloth. This is a test of memory, and the idea is to write down the names of as many objects as you can remember. Finally, you check the tray of objects to see how accurate you were. At first, your score may well be low – only five or six correct. But with practice this increases to eighteen or nineteen, at which point you should try to remember details about the objects rather than just what they are.

Another exercise designed for a similar purpose is 'Directed Attention' – a simple exercise in which the aim is to direct your whole attention on to whatever you are doing at any one time. This may sound silly, but if you make an effort to notice where your attention lies next time you are, shall we say, driving the car, brushing your teeth, washing the dishes, or even tying your shoelaces, you will see the point. We very rarely direct our whole attention on to the task in hand. But such restriction of mental activity is desirable during psychometric readings, and this exercise is the easiest way to learn how to do it. We can note in passing that although the exercise is simple, it forms a part of many systems for the development of psychic ability.

The third exercise oriented to these ends is similar to the first one described above. The idea is to develop your skill in remembering details of an object from brief glimpses of it. The point is this: the more you perceive at a glance, the less time you need to appreciate and understand something. (Notice that although these exercises are carried out in the physical world, with our five physical senses, they develop skills of perception and cognition which assist us in our psychic work. This is further confirmation that our system of perception is the same for psychic sensory input and 'normal' sensory input.) So, while walking or driving or going through your normal daily routine, make an effort to notice (without staring!) the details of people and places around you. You can develop your own system for doing this.

We now come to the other ability which psychometrists need to develop – that of presenting information coherently and accurately. W.E. Butler maintains that success in this basically descriptive technique is essential if you wish to practise psychometry. In his words, once again, 'What is important is the gradual building up of an automatic sequence of attention, so that all the details [of impressions from the sense organs] are stored in their correct pigeon-holes in the subconscious, from which they can be drawn in the same sequence.' Butler suggests that the following general sequence is used to describe individuals:

(1)   estimated height and build of person perceived, together with any outstanding peculiarities
(2)   clothing style and colour
(3)   quick detailed description of features, any peculiarities being noted and described first
(4)   any finer points of identification, mannerisms and so on.

The same principles apply to landscapes and general surroundings. But, it is to be noted, these *are* only principles. You can adapt them to suit your own individual style and experience. Once again, the principles of observation and perception in the physical world also apply to the psychic world. At this point we can assume that you have practised these exercises for a short time and that you are ready to try psychometry itself – although, of course, you can do the exercises and try psychometry concurrently.

Your first choice of an object for a psychometric reading is an important one. Remember that the psychic faculty is actually very subtle and sensitive. For example, there is a danger of confusing past and present information. So even if you consciously want to receive as many impressions as possible about an object, the end result of choosing an object with a complicated history will be confusion. You might prefer to choose an object which has had only one owner, and which has been regularly handled by him. To obtain this, it is quite likely that you will have to call on the assistance of a third party. If you do, ask him to handle the object as little as possible, so that he does not interfere with impressions left on the object by the owner. If you are using an object with a complex history, you may like to choose one which has one particularly strong 'memory layer'. This might represent a period in the object's history which far outweighs all the others in importance. In cases like these, most of the impressions you receive will come from this one period of the object's history.

Necklaces are acknowledged by all psychometrists as good objects for a reading. This is because of their close association with one person. W.E. Butler also suggests that the inside surfaces of letters (not in their envelopes) and gloves are acceptable articles. You should also try pens, watches and diaries – in fact, any small article of personal significance. You can pass on to more complicated readings as you become more expert. So, having selected your article, you are ready to begin. Psychometry, like all psychic techniques, is much more effective if you are at the alpha level. If you have tried the exercises described in Chapter 3, this will be a matter of course to you. If you have not, then you can close your eyes and use five deep breaths to relax and clear your mind. In all cases, you will be sitting comfortably with the object close at hand. Once you feel sufficiently relaxed and receptive, you should make a conscious decision that you are going to achieve successful psychic reception of information. You may either touch the object lightly with the fingers of both hands or bring it up to your forehead (an area which is supposed by some to be the psychic centre of the mind and body). The trick is to keep your calm and receptive frame of mind while allowing impressions to filter through from your subconscious to your conscious mind.

Strictly speaking, 'impressions' are defined as vague feelings. However, I am using the term to cover anything which comes into your awareness during psychometry. There are actually only a few different ways in which this can happen:

(1)   as though they were your own thoughts, but arising quite suddenly and unexpectedly
(2)   as vivid mental pictures or sounds (perceptions)
(3)   as vague, ill-defined feelings or sensations.

It is often helpful to record these impressions for analysis later. You can do this by telling an assistant what you are sensing, so that he can make notes. Alternatively, you may relate your impressions into a tape recorder. In either case, you can later check and confirm the accuracy of the impressions you have obtained.

The particular form in which an individual becomes consciously aware of psychically received information probably depends on a whole range of factors. Most people, though, consciously experience a mixture of thoughts, perceptions and feelings; and it is not possible to state categorically that any one form is predominant to the others. Vivid mental *perceptions* are obviously the easiest to describe, because we are so used to describing things that we have seen or heard in everyday life. Interestingly, some visual or aural perceptions received during psychic work – especially after you have gained a certain amount of experience – are more vivid than perceptions made by means of the five physical senses. Quite frequently, impressions of this type are meaningless to the psychometrist himself, but have some particular significance for the person who owns the object or requested the reading. Jean Burns describes how one Californian psychic received an impression of an orange tree, growing from seed to fruit-bearing maturity, during a reading.[2] Although he felt that this must be irrelevant, he described the mental picture to his clients. They were delighted! They told him they were considering whether to buy an orange grove or some other piece of land. In general, when a psychometrist receives a vivid mental picture of a place, it usually turns out to be somewhere which was (or is) of major significance to a past (or present) owner of an object. Sometimes this appears to be impossible. For example, suppose you were 'reading' an object and an impression of your own house came to mind. There might be some connection between your house and the house of the object's owner. You should not exercise judgement on whatever impressions you receive: simply acknowledge and report them. You can try to understand their significance later.

The next easiest impressions to describe are the ill-defined *feelings* which may come over you. Your aim is to recognize and acknowledge these sensations without letting your consciousness be overcome by them. At this point, we must digress slightly and consider this in greater detail. There is a possibility that you will 'take on' feelings or emotions associated with the history of an object. If this is so, when you begin to use your clairvoyant faculty to pick up information, you could be swamped by sorrow, anger or pain connected with the object. (Something closely related to this effect, which may help you to understand it better, is the sense of calm and peace one sometimes feels in a church.) Although such reception of impressions is a vital part of the psychometric process, it is not helpful to allow your own emotions to be controlled by impressions originating with the object of study. Fortunately, there are two ways of protecting yourself. First, you can learn to control your own emotional reactions. We tend to think of states of mind such as anger or anxiety as beyond conscious control or invention. But this is quite wrong. No matter how annoying, irritating or upsetting you may find something now, you can learn to sit quietly and attentively without it arousing any emotion whatsoever. Emotional reactions are learned; they can be unlearned, with the aid of a conscious decision to act rationally rather than emotionally. However, the emotional habits of a lifetime are not undone quickly, and most people find the second method rather easier: simply make a conscious decision not to take on any emotional reactions associated with the object.

Let us return now to a hypothetical psychometric reading. Suppose you are holding an object and you begin to identify a feeling of unhappiness. Quickly try to discover why this feeling exists. For example, does a memory of any of your own experiences come to mind? If it does, it will bear some relation to the experience of the owner of the object. On a more general level, you may simply be receiving impressions about the general character and personality of this person. Is the owner happy or sad? Relaxed or anxious? Calm or angry? And so on. Feelings about the personality of any individual connected with the object you are holding are especially useful because they can be checked later.

In his discussion of psychometry, W.E. Butler makes a valuable point of warning: information about the ill-health of the owner of an object may be so strongly induced by the object that you actually begin to feel the sensations of the illness as though it were your own. You can use the psychic shield technique described in the chapter on healing (Chapter 12) to prevent this. And, as mentioned before, you can also consciously choose not to take on these sensations. This you will do by mentally saying: 'I choose not to feel these sensations.' Remember, they are not yours, and you do not need to accept them.

Finally, what of *thoughts* that come into the mind? This category of impression is the one most likely to suffer primary process distortion. It is also the one most likely to be dismissed by you as irrelevant during a reading. I have suggested in a previous chapter that many of the intuitive flashes and random thoughts which pass through our minds are actually psychically received information coming into consciousness. Although it can be difficult to distinguish between psychic thoughts and those of no importance, there are two ways of trying to do so. The first is objective: record everything that comes to mind and analyse it later – the correct statements will stand out when you go through your record with someone who can vouch for its accuracy. The second is subjective: pay special attention to any thoughts which are persistent or recurrent.

Quite often, the budding psychometrist is unable to distinguish between the information which he has received psychically and that which has originated in his own mind. In an attempt to avoid inaccuracy, he then becomes over-critical and mentally tense. As we have seen, this will prevent the passage of any information from subconscious to conscious. The problem can be avoided by mentally asking suitable questions about the object or its owner. The answer will be the first impression, thought or feeling which comes into your mind, no matter how silly or irrelevant it may seem. Such questions are best posed pictorially, in the manner described in the chapter on dowsing.

During the early stages of your work, your accuracy will not be high. Two or three statements correct out of ten would be considered good. But surely this is astonishing enough? I cannot emphasize sufficiently that the key to success lies in persistence. You could consider yourself successful when your persistence has led to a level of accuracy approaching eight or nine statements correct out of ten. At this point, you may feel able to dispense with the formality of checking your results. Perhaps it has occurred to you that this level of ability opens up the possibility of using an object to gain information about a person in his absence. It is up to you to see that you maintain a sound set of ethical and moral standards in such work. Further, there will perhaps be occasions when you feel it better not to reveal information that you have received. Suppose you were to obtain an impression of death, sorrow or illness during a reading. It would be unfair to reveal this to the person concerned if you felt that it related to the future rather than the past. In any case, there are enough uncertainties about this kind of psychic work to prevent you from being sure that your impressions are correct.

It is not difficult to find many applications for psychometric techniques. For example, W.E. Butler suggests that the basic method can be modified to distinguish fake antiques or jewels from real ones, to diagnose illness and to pick up impressions about the activities of people around you. Clearly, to develop such abilities needs a considerable amount of experience. I personally prefer to use a dowsing pendulum as a means of receiving information on matters like the ones mentioned above. This is because a dowsing tool allows psychic impressions to be directly displayed by subconsciously controlled muscle movements without any interference or primary process distortion in the conscious mind.

I shall now describe an experiment which can bring home to you more clearly the nature of the faculties with which you are dealing. You will need the assistance of a friend. Ask him or her to obtain five identical objects, such as five pieces of wood of equal size. They should be a convenient size and shape so they can be held in the hand. Your assistant will mark each one with a letter from A to E and then 'charge' it with a particular emotion. This is done by picking up the objects one at a time and visualizing a mental image that relates to the chosen emotion. It is better if he or she can also manage to *feel* that particular emotion while he handles the object. The more energy put into this, the better it will work. Each object is charged with one different emotion. To ensure that the different emotions do not interfere with each other, your assistant should relax for fifteen minutes after charging each object. You can then attempt to psychometrize each object, directing your efforts towards picking up only the relevant emotion. The results will probably astound you. Clearly, there is a (remote) possibility that you will pick up information about the emotion corresponding to each object by telepathic communication with your assistant. However, this cannot be avoided. It is useful to note that this exercise can develop your ability to direct your attention to one particular aspect of an object during a psychometric reading. In cases where an object has a long and complicated history, this could mean the difference between success and failure.

Finally, what of the 'interference' between cards in the card-guessing tests described in the last chapter? This is an effect which, as you have probably realized, is also common during psychometry. It results, quite simply, from the non-specific nature of an undeveloped or untrained psychic sense. In other words, you receive information from a broader spectrum of material than you are aiming for. But practice very quickly enables you to direct your psychic sense on to the particular problem with which you are concerned. (We shall consider the mechanism behind all forms of ESP, including clairvoyant and precognitive psychometry, in Chapters 10 and 14.)

REFERENCES

1. W.E. Butler, *How to Develop Psychometry* (Aquarian Press, Wellingborough, 1973).
2. Jean Burns, *Your Innate Psychic Powers* (Sphere, London, 1981), p. 64.

8.

Water Divining and Other Dowsing

Most people probably think of dowsing as 'water divining'. This term has passed out of use because one can find far more than water by using a dowsing rod or pendulum: oil, minerals, buried objects, missing people, and so on. The list is endless. There are experiments described in this chapter and the next which will enable you to discover which of these techniques interests you the most. And you should try the exercises, because dowsing is easy and simple. This can make it a useful starting point for the development of psychic ability for those people who are, shall we say, sceptical by nature!

In dowsing, as in all psychic techniques, we are obtaining information which is hidden from the normal senses through the use of our psychic faculties. This time, however, any information received is exposed to view with the aid of a tool such as a forked twig, angle rod or a pendulum. Most frequently, dowsing is used in the field as one walks over the ground. Sometimes, however, a dowser will use a map of the area which he wishes to search. (This map, or 'distant', dowsing is explained in the next chapter.) Other dowsers specialize in finding missing people; some even try to diagnose illness at a distance.

Dowsing is probably a form of clairvoyance. Thus, in theory, you could use it to obtain any information which you require. In practice, however, there are advantages in knowing something about the objective of each search. This is a short cut, so that when searching for oil, say, you start by searching an area geologically likely to produce it. Clearly, certain areas do not contain oil, and it would be a waste of time to look for it there. Perhaps by now you are beginning to have some doubts. If you were not aware of the different uses to which dowsing can be put, it may be looking less and less plausible. To overcome these doubts, I shall first of all describe how you can try it for yourself. Most people find that dowsing works the first time they try it. This is proof positive of the reality of dowsing in particular, and of psychic ability in general.

How to dowse

You will need to start by obtaining the correct tools. For a beginner, the *angle rods* are probably easiest to use. To make these, any two pieces of metal rod about $\frac{1}{8}$ inch (3 mm) in diameter and 24 inches (60 cm) long will be satisfactory. The metal should be bent to form an angle rod with two arms at 90° to each other, the shorter being about 6 inches (15 cm) long. The base and part of one side of a metal coat-hanger will make a good angle rod if the shorter side is bent at an angle of 90° to the base. Some authorities on dowsing have suggested that better results are obtained if the short arm is placed in a holder, such as the empty case of a ballpoint pen, and the holder is then grasped in the fist. I have never found this necessary and I would not recommend it, because if the ground where you are working is slightly bumpy, or the wind strong, the rods tend to move independently of the dowsing reaction. You will probably be quite successful if you hold the angle rods (one in each hand) with the short end grasped loosely in the fist with the long arm pointing forward, parallel to the ground.

Your arms should be comfortable, with the upper arms straight downwards by the side of your body and the forearms held parallel to the ground in front of your body. You may place your thumbs lightly on the bends in the rods to stop excessive movements caused by wind or the unevenness of the ground. When the dowsing reaction occurs it will be quite distinctive, and you need have no fear of preventing the rods moving. Opinion varies as to the degree of tension you should have in your arms. General J. Scott Elliot, who is an acknowledged expert on dowsing, recommends having the upper arms hanging loosely by the sides;[1] however, since the dowsing experience is primarily a personal one, I would be reluctant to make such a definite statement. On my first attempt I pressed my arms firmly into the sides of my body and this seemed to work quite well. Indeed, there may be a sound reason for this: it appears that the subconscious muscle movements responsible for dowsing may be greater if there is already some tension in the arms.

Most people identify dowsing with the *forked twig*, even

though it is not as suitable for beginners, because a much stronger response is needed to give a movement. However, when a strong response *is* obtained, the twig twists upwards or downwards in the hands of the operator with such force that he may appear to be fighting it. My advice would be: start with the angle rods, and use them until you have identified and cultivated the dowsing response. In this way, you will avoid any problems which might be caused by the need for greater skill when using the forked twig. It is true that a few people know clearly and positively, from the first time they hold a dowsing rod, that they are natural dowsers. Such people might be able to start with the forked twig. For example, in my own family one of my brothers had no reaction on his first attempt while another was an expert from the word 'go'. I think one of them failed because his mental attitude was not correct − we will return to this in a moment. The point is that if you are slightly sceptical on your first attempt, you are much more likely to suceed with the angle rods than with the forked twig. However, if you are really determined, this is how you could try the forked twig.

Traditionally, forked twigs are made from hazel, apple or peach. In reality, as long as the twig is springy, the type of wood is not particularly important. Unfortunately, each time the wood dries out and becomes brittle, you will have to cut a new twig. You are aiming to obtain a tool which can be put under tension by holding the two long arms of the V apart. In fact, this is not as simple as it sounds. Whether or not a dowsing reaction is obtained depends upon the length and thickness of the arms of the V, and also the angle between them. So probably the best way of deciding which twigs will do is to try several until you find one you are happy with. Normally the arms of the V will be at least 20 inches (50 cm) long, as symmetrical as you can find, with the end part where they joint about 3 inches (80 mm) long. The thinnest part of each arm of the V should be flexible, probably about $\frac{1}{4}$ inch (6 mm) in diameter.

Once again, the upper arms are held vertical with the forearms parallel to the ground in front of the body. The palms face upwards, and the end of one side of the V is grasped with the fingers of each hand. This means that the wood is flexed through a right angle and protrudes out of the clenched fists with the thumbs pressing on the very ends. You can have the main body of the fork pointing upwards, downwards or out in front of you when you start: most commonly, the twig is pointing downwards to search and moves upwards (away from the body) when the response is obtained. A small amount of tension will be needed to make the twig respond correctly; you can achieve this by pulling sideways and backwards slightly to place the twig in an unstable equilibrium. (Before going on to describe the different responses and search techniques, I should mention that there are many other dowsing tools. The pendulum is generally used for map dowsing and similar activities; for work in the field, besides the angle rods and the forked twig, you might find wands, nylon V rods and even dowsers who use their hands alone. However, it is my belief that if people develop sufficient skill and interest in dowsing, they will research the subject themselves to find out all they wish to know and so these other approaches need not concern us here.[2])

Having obtained the tools, you are now ready to dowse for the first time. Perhaps a little sceptical, you will certainly need to feel the dowsing response from a known source, so that you can recognize it again when trying to locate a hidden source. The best place to start is with water running underground, because there is a wealth of accumulated experience from which to learn and interpret the results. I suggest that you work in a field which you know to be drained or over an underground stream of which you know the course. You can then try the 'stream test'. Before I describe this, however, there are one or two other points which I want to make.

Some years ago, when I was at university, I watched the agriculture students being shown dowsing as a method of locating underground drainage systems. Using angle rods made from welding rods, they tried to detect the layout of porous clay pipes forming a herring-bone drainage system in a wet, marshy field. On their first attempts, almost 90 per cent of the students were able to dowse with a fair degree of accuracy. Perhaps surprisingly, amongst a group of intellectual students who might be expected to question an activity which falls outside normal scientific experience, there was total acceptance of the results. You will find that the same sort of attitude (that is, open acceptance of the procedure as something which works and does not necessarily need explanation) will help you to succeed as well. Do try and keep preconceived ideas out of your mind. If you expect or try to get particular results while dowsing, you may find that you are consciously moving the tool and so misleading yourself. (This is not the same as *knowing* that you should get a result in the stream test.)

Because dowsing is a psychic technique, it is easier to be successful if you are in a quiet, alpha state. If you have practised relaxation and visualization regularly, you will find it easy to stay in alpha with your eyes open as you dowse. But dowsing, as I have already mentioned, seems to work for most people anyway. It is as though the very act of dowsing 'forces' you into the correct level of mind. Here is a description of the state of mind in which most successful dowsers work. It is taken from Francis Hitching's book, *Pendulum: the Psi Connection:*

> . . . it involves a series of paradoxes and contradictions, a balance between two opposing moods. You have to concentrate on what you are looking for, but at the same time be relaxed and uninvolved. . . . It has been compared to a mild state of hypnosis, or trance, or meditation; and certainly most dowsers, even if they talk to you, when they are working, give the appearance of having temporarily removed part of their mind from normal consciousness. It is a state that involves harmony, instinct and simplicity. Another adjective used is 'receptive' . . . some part of your mind, deep down, always knows what you are looking for. . . . As long as you settle your mind into a state where it is comfortably receptive, the reaction will happen anyway.[3]

There is little to choose between visualizing an image of what you are looking for, such as an underground stream, or posing a mental 'question' such as: 'Please indicate when I am directly over water.' However, if you wish to determine the depth and flow rate of water, you will certainly need to pose questions mentally, so it might be useful to start learning and develop with this one technique. Essentially, though, you must try these experiences for yourself and concentrate on whatever works best. Dowsing is a very personal experience! Someone once said to me, 'Well, who do you ask for an indication that you've found what you're looking for?' So note that you are not asking the question of a person: it is merely a way of consciously setting your subconscious psychic faculty to work.

The importance of having your objective clearly in mind was brought home to me once when I was showing a friend how to dowse field drains like the ones I mentioned earlier. In 1976, when Britain was in the grip of the worst drought for over a hundred years, I could not obtain a response as I moved over the ground, mentally 'asking' the rods to indicate when water was flowing under my feet. Only after several failures did I realize that I should have been thinking, 'Please indicate when I am directly over a drain pipe' because, of course, they were dry and no water was flowing through them.

The stream test

First of all, try and cultivate the attitude described above. Then, form a mental image or pose a question relating to your target. Next, walk slowly towards your target. For a beginner, the rods will often move together coming up to the target, and cross when you are past it; but do not worry if you miss it, because your accuracy will improve with time. At this stage, the dowsing reaction itself is more important – an opinion that you are likely to share when you experience it. If you are using the angle rods you will probably think they have a life of their own and there may even be an overwhelming sensation that some arcane power is moving them. In fact this can be awe-inspiring, but it is quite wrong; the angle rods move because of minute muscle movements produced by the subconscious which twist the arms one way or the other. Some dowsers (myself included) prefer to hold the rods in the bare hands rather than to use a holder because the feel on one's palms is quite distinctive – a tingling sensation, often very noticeable. I presume this is due to increased perspiration, which in turn is another sign of the subconscious at work.

The movement of the forked twig is somewhat puzzling. From the search position it moves upwards or downwards, sometimes with such strength that it twists out of the hands of the dowser. If minute muscle movements are causing this, they must be very powerful indeed! But despite the incomplete explanation of the movement, the response clearly indicates when the search object is found – and perhaps that is all we need to know?

On any future occasion when you need to use dowsing techniques, you can follow the same basic procedure. That is, you walk across the ground in which you expect to locate your target, with the dowsing rod in the search position. As you do so, mentally ask a question or form an image of the target. If the target lies in the area you are searching, the dowsing reaction will show you where. There are several refinements of technique which you can use to obtain far more information about your target. For example, if you wish to determine the depth of water accurately, the technique is easily adapted: you stand over the water with the tool in the normal search position and count downwards. You might mentally ask: 'Please indicate when I reach the depth at which the water may be found. Is the water at ten feet? ... twenty? ... thirty?' and so on. However, this does take some skill, and my advice would be that if you wish to obtain such information, you should first find water with the angle rods and then use the pendulum to determine its depth and flow rate. This is because the pendulum is much more suited to constant questioning – and gives a 'yes' and 'no' type reaction, which enables questioning to take the easier form of: 'Is the water more than ten feet down? ... twenty feet down? ... thirty feet down?' etc. Experts agree that the angle rod can be used to give a yes/no reaction (where no is the 'search' position, and yes is the 'found'), but the technique is not as sensitive.

You will find that the dowsing reaction varies according to what you are searching for. The angle rods may swing inwards or outwards, and the forked twig up or down. Furthermore, different people using the same tool in the same place will obtain a different response – with the forked twig, sometimes a swing upwards and sometimes downwards. As long as you know which result is a positive reaction for you, the actual direction is unimportant.

Once you are satisfied with the basic response, you will probably wish to extend your technique. You can do this by using your skill (which will now continue to develop) to locate minerals or specific objects such as water pipes, gas mains, electricity cables and hidden objects, or by determining the depth and flow rate of a stream once it has been found. Perhaps the best known case of dowsing for hidden objects was that of the US Marines in Vietnam, who located hidden mines and the treacherous trenches in which the Vietcong used to hide. This came about through Louis Matacia, a Virginia dowser, who demonstrated his ability to locate these hidden tunnels on a Marine base in the United States, mapping them with such skill and accuracy that when the combat troops heard of it, they adopted the same techniques (unofficially) for use under battle conditions.[4]

I have suggested that the pendulum can be used to give a yes/no indication when you are dowsing. But, in fact, its uses are much wider than that. In the next chapter, therefore, we shall examine some of these applications, and also look at other ways in which you can practise dowsing.

REFERENCES AND NOTES

1   J. Scott Elliot, *Dowsing: One Man's Way* (Neville Spearman, 1977), p. 39.
2   Two of the best general reference books on the whole field of dowsing, which contain much information on all these points, are F. Hitching, *Pendulum: the Psi Connection* (Fontana, London, 1977), and P. Underwood, *The Complete Book of Dowsing and Divining* (Rider, London, 1980).
3   Hitching, op. cit., pp. 74–5.
4   This well-known example of the use of dowsing is described in Hitching, op. cit., p. 65.

9.

The Pendulum and Its Uses in Dowsing

I hope that, by now, you have had the opportunity of trying dowsing for yourself. You may have decided, however, to read the book through before experimenting, and if this is so, you will have had no reinforcing experience to guide you through this chapter. You should suspend your critical instinct and read the chapter in the same spirit as I suggested you should adopt for your first dowsing test – open acceptance.

The pendulum is a tool that extends the dowsing field considerably, both in terms of the information available from the instrument, and also the psychic experience of the investigator. I shall start by describing the pendulum itself. Most experienced dowsers use a short length of thread – nylon fishing line would be ideal, or sewing cotton if it is not available – on the end of which is tied a bob made from some simple small weight such as a key or lead fishing weight. It is often claimed that the thread should be about 3 or 4 inches (7.5 cm) long, so as to give quick gyrations; however, I much prefer a longer thread of about 10 inches (25 cm). Although this means that the work takes longer, I seem to get better results. When using a pendulum, one generally sits (preferably at a table) with the work nearby. This is often a map or sheet of paper. The thread is held between the tips of the forefinger and thumb, with any excess wrapped around the other fingers well away from the pendulum. The forearm should be parallel to the table with the pendulum bob about 6 inches (12.5 cm) above the table top.

The most important aspect of using a pendulum is to establish a code which will allow you to interpret the information you receive when dowsing. To do this, place an electric light on the table and switch it on. Hold the pendulum over the cable and mentally ask the question, 'Is there current flowing in this cable?' As you do this, you should try to attain the detached but observant attitude described in the last chapter. Whichever direction the pendulum swings when the light is on means 'yes'; whichever direction it swings when the light is off means 'no'. Do ensure that you leave enough time between your questions to allow the swing to alter its movement. Most people find that 'yes' is indicated by a clockwise swing, and 'no' by an anticlockwise swing. But do not worry if your responses are directly reversed. You may even obtain a swing which is simply in one plane; for example, 'no' may be indicated by a back and forward motion. Perhaps I should emphasize that the pendulum does not move on its own. *You* make it swing; but you do so with muscle movements which are controlled by the part of your mind with psychic sensitivity. In other words, do not consciously try to decide which way the pendulum will swing. Simply allow minute movements of your hand or fingers to occur; if you are in the right frame of mind, those movements will be controlled by your psychic faculty.

By conducting this simple test on the light cable, you will be able to establish your own code for all future work. Thus we can see that the pendulum is an instrument which is used mainly to answer questions 'yes' or 'no'. Sometimes, however, it is used without reference to the code. In such circumstances, you would probably be trying to detect a variation in the environmental situation. I have given some examples of tests like these later in the book, but I can quickly illustrate the idea with two simple exercises at this point. For the first one, you will need a map showing part of the coast. Hold the pendulum over the sea, and watch the direction of swing which seems most natural. Then, without altering the position of the hand which is holding the pendulum, ask someone to move the map until the land is underneath the bob. Surprised? As a second example of this use of the pendulum, try to find the odd coin amongst four similar ones placed in a shallow tray of sand. Move the pendulum across the tray until the direction of swing changes. While doing this you should have the thought, 'Please indicate when I am over the odd coin' in your mind. Obviously tests like these do not involve the use of a yes/no code. However, let us return to the code now. The first time I tried to use a pendulum, the reaction was so convincing that I immediately went on to try and find a hidden key. You may like to do this yourself.

Select some small article, say a key, and ask a member of

your family to place it somewhere in the house without revealing where. Hold the pendulum as described earlier and mentally pose the question, 'Is the key upstairs?' Assuming the answer is yes, the sequence of questions might be as follows: 'Is it in the large bedroom?' Answer: No. 'Is it in the small bedroom?' Answer: No. 'Is it in the bathroom?' Answer: Yes. 'Is it under the carpet?' Answer: No. 'Is it in the wall cabinet?' Answer: Yes. 'Is it on the top shelf?' Answer: No. 'Is it on the bottom shelf?' Answer: Yes. Probably you will find that at such an early stage this will not always work out correctly for you. Even so, I have met several people who had no success with the dowsing rods yet were exceptionally successful on their first attempt with the pendulum, so do not be surprised if it works!

Of course any question can be put to the pendulum, even ones on apparently trivial topics such as asking whether the weather will be fine at the weekend if you are planning to go out. (Immediately the pendulum has gained another use. It is now a divination system − a means of foretelling the future. This emphasizes the link between all psychic techniques.) In his book *Modern Dowsing*, Raymond Willey describes how a dowser located a fault in some telephone cables by counting upwards while asking how many poles along the line from his house the fault would be found. When he reached a certain number, the pendulum indicated 'yes'. When this was checked, the fault was actually found to be at the place indicated by the dowser.[1] However, for your own practice, nothing so complicated is needed. Instead, you can ask questions like: 'Has the mail been delivered yet?' or, 'Will any visitors call today?' (If the answer is yes, try to find out who it is.) or even 'How many plates are there in the left hand stack in the cupboard? Is it ten? ... eleven? ... twelve?' and so on.

While asking the question you will probably find that your attention is wandering. Do not be disturbed by this: simply bring it back to the matter in hand. Francis Hitching makes a valuable point when he mentions that beginners frequently have difficulty in dowsing because they are easily embarrassed and distracted.[2] However, the only cure for these problems is plenty of practice, and the early successes will increase your confidence and ability. But, most important of all, you should be aware that you must pose clear and unambiguous questions. If you are using the yes/no code, for example, and find that the pendulum swing is not too well defined, then it may be that your question cannot be answered 'yes' or 'no'. There is also another reason for asking precise questions. Occasionally, you will receive a dowsing signal about an object's position even when the object has been moved from your search area. This is called 'remanence' and seems to be a kind of precognition in reverse: you pick up information about events in the past. For example, I was dowsing a sketch map of a friend's house after he had phoned me and asked me to locate a lost book. I obtained three responses, one of which showed where the book in question was lost. The second showed a place where it had been kept in the past, and the third showed a place where books were habitually located on shelves. To avoid remanence as far as possible, keep your questions specific: for example, 'Is *my present front* door key located in this area *now*?'

Here are some more suggestions for practice, given by J. Scott Elliot.[3]

(1)   Take three or more cups. Put water or a coin in one; cover them up and seek the one with the water or coin.

(2)   Get someone to hide an object in the bookcase. Work along with the pendulum until you find it.

(3)   Ask someone to obtain a leaf. Try to identify the plant it came from.

(4)   Plot the routes of the drains, electric cables and water pipes of your own house, and the houses of your friends.

(5)   Have a friend fill three containers with similar looking liquids, such as weak coffee, tea and meat essence (or water, salt solution and sugar solution) and mark them, before you identify them.

Map dowsing with a pendulum

Pendulum dowsing seems more mysterious than ordinary dowsing because one can conduct a search for a particular object using only a map of the target area – even if this happens to be on the other side of the globe. But there is no doubt that map dowsing really works: the number of reported successes is so large. The technique itself is actually quite simple. One starts with a small scale map (perhaps even a map of the world) and narrows down the field of search by using the pendulum to answer questions about the location of the search object. As the area is located more and more precisely, a larger and larger scale map must be used, until eventually the final pin-pointing is done with a sketch map. A grid is drawn over the sketch map using some natural feature of the area such as a road or railway line as a base. The relation between the real object and the landmark is then the same as that between the position of the dowsing reaction and the position of the landmark on the sketch map. However, some dowsers think accuracy demands that one should go out into the field to do the final location. My objection to that is purely practical – you may not be able to go to the area to which your search refers. Here is an example of a case like this.

Early in 1973 J. Scott Elliot decided to produce an oil map of the North Sea. (This was before the major explorations had taken place.) He was trying to identify areas where oil might be found, and to give an idea of its depth and ease of extraction. His method involved drawing a map of the search area at a scale just large enough to show the oil fields. Once this had been done, he moved the pendulum backwards and forwards across the map while thinking: 'Please indicate when I am over the edge of an oil field.' The oil fields were so large that this method enabled him to draw their size and position.

As J. Scott Elliot has written, map dowsing enables a dowser to study the ground or seas in any part of the world without leaving home and with all his facilities to hand.[4] The technique is as versatile as normal dowsing, and as many objects can be located with it. Preferably there should be the possibility of later checking (although this happened some years later with the oil map!) so that the dowser's confidence in his own ability can be maintained. At this point you are probably wondering how accurate the oil map turned out to be. Examination of the results, which can be found in Scott Elliot's book, *Dowsing: One Man's Way*,[5] shows that he pin-pointed several areas where oil companies later had major strikes. This could not be ascribed to chance, because he plotted few areas where oil has not been found.

If you try map dowsing yourself, your first step should always be to narrow down the area which you have to search. For example, a large map should be split into smaller areas and the pendulum used to find out whether the object being sought is within those boundaries. Remember that your question should be very precise: ask whether your target exists in that part of the world represented by the map *at the present time*. Assuming that the initial enquiry with the map and pendulum shows an area where the target is located, you will be in a position to proceed on a very large scale map. This will probably be a sketch map which you have drawn yourself. If the target is large compared to the scale of the map (as in the case of Scott Elliot's oil map) then you could draw a grid on the map and dowse each square for the target. However, this does tend to be rather laborious. A better method is to use the 'directional and distance' search.[6] This is the method. You sit at a table with the map in front of you and move a finger down a line drawn on the left hand side of the map while mentally asking: 'Does the object lie on a line running East/West through this point?' As soon as your finger hits the point through which the East/West co-ordinates of the object pass, the pendulum swing will change. Mark this point. Then find the North/South co-ordinate by running your finger across a line drawn at the top of the map, asking: 'Does the object lie on a line running North/South through this point?' Draw intersecting lines through these points; where they cross will indicate the location of the object. Since you may overshoot, it is wise to double check by running your finger in the reverse direction each time while asking the same questions. If the two reactions in each axis are in a slightly different place, midway between them represents the spot you are searching for.

That, then, is the essence of dowsing. In case after case, experienced and novice dowsers obtain results which show beyond question that this psychic experience is available to everyone. The inconsistencies between dowsers lie with their techniques, and perhaps also the feelings which they experience while dowsing. These variations do not tell us anything what-soever about the mechanism of dowsing. However, we can make a few observations. Any theory which explains dowsing must also be able to explain clairvoyance; it must be able to account for the fact that everyone can dowse, given the right mental attitude; it must acknowledge that dowsing is independent of distance; and it must explain remanence.

In the next chapter, we shall examine the relationship between science and dowsing and ESP. Later in the book I shall attempt to show how science and ESP can be brought together. But before any of this, you may wish to practise your dowsing skills. Here are some more exercises in dowsing which should enable you to do just that.

Other exercises in dowsing

(1)　When you are standing in open country, why not try to determine where the nearest water is located by using a directional search through 360 degrees (a full circle) while asking mentally: 'In which direction will water be found?' When the rods move, you are facing the right way. You can then try counting to find out how far away it is.

(2)　Francis Hitching reports that Japanese farmers use dowsers to sex young chicks, a job which is otherwise impossible to do accurately! You can adapt this application of dowsing to tell a mother-to-be whether her child is a boy or girl. In this test, you should hold the pendulum over the mother's abdomen and double check, by asking, 'Is this baby going to be a boy?' and then, 'Is this baby going to be a girl?' Make sure that you have established your yes/no response code before you start!

(3)　Why not astonish your friends and family by plotting their movements for one day on a sketch map? If you are emotionally close to someone, you will find that the accuracy you achieve is about 100 per cent right.

(4)　You could try asking the pendulum whether a journey will be safe before you set out. If you are planning to fly, and the response indicates some danger, only you can decide whether your accuracy is such that you should postpone your trip. You may find that, as with the *I Ching* (see Chapter 11), it is wiser to be guided by your psychic sense.

(5)　Hold the pendulum over food or drink, and find out whether it is good for you. (If the response is indeterminate, this means 'neither good nor bad'.) Sometimes this can have surprising results.

(6)　Any other test you can think up. Perhaps one day a competition winner will not claim his success is due to skill or luck, but to his ability with the dowsing pendulum!

REFERENCES AND NOTES

1 R. Willey, *Modern Dowsing* (Esoteric Publications, Arizona, 1976).

2 F. Hitching, *Pendulum: the Psi Connection* (Fontana, London, 1977), contains information on all these points. It is a thoroughly researched and comprehensive book, which is probably the beginner's best introduction to the subject.

3 These suggestions were delivered by J. Scott Elliot to the British Society of Dowsers in 1975, and are reported in Hitching, op. cit., p. 79. I have reworded and shortened them slightly.

4 J. Scott Elliot, *Dowsing: One Man's Way* (Neville Spearman, 1977), p. 52.

5 Elliot, op. cit., Part II, Section 8, contains details of the method and results of this case.

6 See Hitching, op. cit., p. 89.

10.

Can Science Explain
ESP and Dowsing?

Most scientists do not consider psychic phenomena worthy of explanation. Their logic is that ESP appears to contravene the scientific laws which govern our existence, and so ESP cannot exist. You cannot investigate and explain non-existent phenomena! Even the experimental results obtained by Rhine and others have been ignored by most and derided by many.

When a scientist goes beyond straightforward attempts to demonstrate ESP and starts trying to explain it, he has basically two choices. He may try to explain ESP within the framework of existing knowledge, or he may propose that existing knowledge is inadequate. Not until the final chapter of the book will I attempt to show how existing knowledge needs to be adapted, expanded and manipulated to explain psychic events. At the moment, we are concerned with the first of the scientist's two options – trying to explain ESP and dowsing in terms of existing knowledge. There have been comparatively few attempts to do this. One reason for this is given above (that ESP breaks scientific laws and so 'cannot' exist). Another reason may be that comparatively few scientists have actually seen laboratory demonstrations of psychic ability. Why should this be so? To understand this, you must first of all understand why laboratory tests are so important to scientists. Science regards quantitative and numerical analysis as essential to defining the properties of any object, event, system or the laws governing that object, event or system. For example, if you investigated the factors which control plant growth, you might find that red light made plants grow faster. To report these experimental results for your fellow scientists to examine and check, you would need to specify a number of things. How much faster? What wavelength of red light? And so on. This is reasonable, of course. And we should not complain when science demands the same repeatable, well-defined experiments on ESP. However, as we have seen, one's attitude of mind is important in determining whether or not one is successful in psychic experiments. This suggests that the rigour of controlled laboratory tests is not an ideal way of generating psychic activity. Perhaps this is why so few scientists have managed to demonstrate psychic work under conditions which satisfy them. If they cannot demonstrate psychic ability, how could they be expected to explain it? Anyway, despite this seemingly intractable and circular problem, let us now review the few attempts which have been made to do this.

The essence of all attempts to explain psychic work in terms of existing and accepted scientific knowledge is simple: by what means does information (unavailable to the normal sense organs) reach the mind during psychic activity? There are, so conventional scientific wisdom tells us, only four possibilities: the four basic forces known to exist in the universe – radioactivity, the atomic forces which hold atoms together, gravitation and electromagnetism. I do not think that radioactivity or atomic forces are regarded by anyone as serious contenders for the transmission of psychically received information. For one thing, they are much too weak and localized. Highly energetic radioactivity is an exception, of course, but it is also totally destructive.

The only theory I have ever seen which involves gravity as an explanation of psychic communication was formed by Dr A. Puharich. He sets his theory out in great detail in his book *Beyond Telepathy*.[1] It is supported by comprehensive calculation and data. As I understand it, a 'psi plasma' field extends throughout the entire universe, surrounding all atomic particles and held close to them by the gravitational field created by their natural spin. The psi plasma field, so the theory goes, will expand when the gravitational force of an object drops, and may then contact other plasma fields from objects further away. Puharich suggests that the human brain undergoes a change in gravitational force when telepathy is experienced. He claims that this drop in gravity is caused by the reduction in frequency of brain waves which is associated with telepathy, the overall effect being to allow the psi plasma field of the receiver to reach that of the sender. The psi plasma field has the property of allowing memory and details of an incident to be transmitted through it, thereby explaining telepathy and ESP. Although the book contains some interesting ideas, in particular his discussion of the physiology of brain waves, this theory seems unnecessarily complicated to me.

All of which leaves us with electromagnetism as a possible agent for the psychic transmission of information. Electromagnetic radiation has two components – electrical energy and magnetism. We need to look closely at magnetism because there have been some suggestions that it plays a major role in dowsing, if not in ESP. The earth acts as a giant magnet, the field strength of which is said to be about half a gauss. (The field strength of a small horseshoe magnet is about 1000 gauss.) This varies in electrical storms, for example, when it decreases by about 100 times. Since this always corresponds to an increase in admissions to psychiatric hospitals, it is clear that sensitivity to this level of magnetism is not especially unusual. Evidence of much greater sensitivity to magnetism becomes apparent when we consider the work of Zaboj Harvalik.[2] He investigated magnetic field sensitivity by using a field produced in his garden from a direct current cable under the soil. It was claimed that he could create a variable field as low as .000 000 0001 gauss. Whether or not this was indeed the case does not matter too much; he clearly was using a very weak magnetic field barely measurable with the best equipment available and only a fraction of the strength of the earth's own field. He asked dowsers to determine by using angle rods whether the field was on or off. (It was on when the current flowed through the cable.) The results seemed clear – everyone could detect changes in the magnetic field.

At first sight, these results seem to show clearly that dowsers are responding to magnetism, because many of the artefacts that can be identified by dowsing, such as water, archaeological remains, tunnels, cables and so on, create magnetic field patterns. When one learns that each type of artefact produces a unique and particular type of magnetic field in a particular three-dimensional pattern, we appear to be home and dry; theoretically one would only need to suggest that a dowser could recognize each three-dimensional pattern, and he would have the ability to identify these underground objects. Unfortunately, this theory will not hold water. Leaving aside the fact that if this were the case, each dowser would in some way already have the magnetic pattern of every possible object that he might be called upon to look for stored in his brain, the experimental results described above are open to question. It may be that the dowsers were actually sensing Harvalik's expectations when the switch was on. If so, they would be working through telepathy, not dowsing. But the strongest objection to any theory involving a magnetic influence on the human mind is that it cannot in any way explain map dowsing or remanence.

You have probably realized that map dowsing is a particular form of clairvoyance and that remanence may well be the opposite of precognition. Thus by eliminating magnetism as an explanation for dowsing, we have also eliminated it as an explanation for ESP. And now we are only left with electromagnetism. If this cannot explain ESP and dowsing, then we must assume that existing scientific knowledge cannot help us! Electromagnetism is, of course, the energy which extends over a whole spectrum from very short wave-length radiation (gamma rays) through X-rays, ultra-violet, light, infra-red, radio waves and finally static electric and magnetic fields. Somewhere in this spectrum there may be a frequency which carries the information picked up by a psychic. This is made slightly more likely by the fact that all bodies in the universe emit electromagnetism (e.m.) and the spectrum is so huge.

At a frequency of 1 cycle per second, the e.m. wavelength is about fifty times the radius of the earth. At the opposite end of the spectrum, gamma rays with a frequency of 10^{22} cycles per second (10^2 is 100, 10^3 is 1000, and so on) have a wavelength so short that a million million placed alongside each other could pass through a space one millimetre wide. Is there any point on this huge spectrum where the waves could be a suitable carrier for telepathic information? We can eliminate certain frequencies at once; their properties obviously make them unsuitable. Anything on the ultra-violet side of visible light has a destructive effect on human tissue (consider X-rays, for example). On the other side of visible light, microwaves will not be suitable because of their cooking effect. We are thus left with a band of radiation extending over frequencies between 1 and 10^9 cycles per second. The wavelength of these waves will be between 300,000 kilometres and 30 centimetres respectively. There is considerable evidence that radiation in this frequency band can affect both humans and animals. For example, people living near radar or defence installations sometimes report that they are troubled by persistent, low-frequency buzzing noises. Interestingly, such frequencies are quite beyond the capacity of the human ear, so the perception of sound must be a result of some interaction between the brain and the electromagnetic radiation. There is other evidence, too; experiments reported by Professor A. Presman of Moscow University suggest that nearly every organ in the body can be affected by electromagnetic radiation.[3] For example, structural changes take place in the brains of rabbits, cats and guinea pigs when they are exposed to bursts of electromagnetic waves at different frequencies; radiation at 2800 cycles per second causes degeneration of rats' testes; monkeys' heart rates are affected by magnetic fields; and so on. The general conclusion must be that electromagnetic sensitivity *does* exist.

But the most compelling evidence comes from experiments by R. Wever, working in Germany. He studied the daily sleep/waking cycles of two groups of men kept in underground bunkers. One group was not shielded from the outside radiation which occurs naturally around the earth. The other, experimental, group was kept in similar bunkers but was shielded as much as possible from electromagnetic radiation. In the shielded bunker the men's sleep/waking cycles were dramatically disturbed. After ten days there was no daily pattern of sleep and waking in common between the men, and they had lost all synchrony with the outside world. When a weak field of 10 cycles per second electromagnetic radiation was applied, all the disturbances were corrected.[4]

Since there is so much evidence that man is sensitive to a wide range of electromagnetic radiation, we must now consider whether it could be responsible for the transmission of the information picked up in psychic work. Consider first of all the 'inverse square law' which governs the transmission of electromagnetic radiation. This states, simply, that the energy emitted from a source decreases in inverse proportion to the square of distance between observer and source: the decrease is rapid, and over a long distance the signal would be literally impossible to distinguish from background signals. But when a psychic is working, he will tell you that there is no noticeable diminution of the signal as he moves away from the source; nor does it get stronger as he approaches it. This fact alone almost eliminates electromagnetic radiation as a possible contender for the information carrier.

There are other lines of reasoning which tend to support this conclusion. In the 1960s a Russian scientist investigated whether telepathy could be transmitted on low frequency e.m. radiation.[5] He worked from theoretical considerations about the amount of information which can be carried by a radio wave in relation to its wavelength and power, and then used established theory to determine the source current which would be needed to propagate such a wave. He discovered that there must be an upper limit to the wavelength of any e.m. radiation being generated by the human body because of the limited energy available. There must also be a lower limit, because the activity of the brain could not produce the very high frequencies associated with low wavelength e.m. radiation. (There is no oscillator working at such enormously high speeds in the human brain.) Various other considerations led him to conclude that only wavelengths of between 300 and 1000 kilometres could be involved with ESP and dowsing. Unfortunately, we know that such wavelengths would produce so little energy in a brain acting as receiver that it would never be noticed. The inescapable conclusion of these observations is this: electromagnetic radiation cannot possibly be the means by which information is transmitted psychically.

Precognition also causes conventional scientific wisdom a great deal of difficulty! Science has an immutable law: that of causality, which states that every effect (or event) has a cause. Precognition and divination are methods of 'seeing' into the future – which implies that the law of causality can be broken. Science holds that it cannot be broken. Considering this together with the above observations on telepathic communication, we come inevitably to a point where conventional scientific wisdom and psychic abilities go their separate ways! But you should not despair – there is a way of explaining psychic work, but we must cover some more ground first. Only when all the threads of our exploration have come together will we be able to approach an understanding. And that is the aim of the final chapter of this book. For the time being, let us note the conflict between science and the psychic world by reflecting on the comments about map dowsing made by Dr Jena Barnothy (a physicist) to Francis Hitching:

> If you tell me that a man can sit on the other side of the Atlantic and look at a map, and receive information about something not shown on the map ... it is impossible. It is outside the laws of physics.[6]

REFERENCES AND NOTES

1   A. Puharich, *Beyond Telepathy* (Souvenir Press, London, 1974).
2   Harvalik's work is described in an obscure journal; a more readily available account is contained in F. Hitching, *Pendulum: the Psi Connection* (Fontana, London, 1977), pp. 115–25.
3   A. Presman, *Electromagnetic Fields and Life* (Plenum Press, New York, 1970).
4   See Hitching, op. cit., p. 138.
5   This work is described in Taylor, *Science and the Supernatural* (Maurice Temple-Smith, London, 1975), pp. 68–9.
6   See Hitching, op. cit., p. 155.

11.

Divination: Foretelling the Future

Divination is a technique which enables one to foretell future events through the use of a mechanical system and explanatory texts. The various divinatory systems available to us today are derived from historical methods which have been more or less modified over the centuries; of these, the one which holds most interest for the West is the *Chinese Book of Change*, or *I Ching* (pronounced 'Yee Jing'). It is one of the oldest books in existence, written in the time of the Chou dynasty over 3000 years ago; despite this, it is as relevant to modern society as it was to ancient China. We shall see why this is so later in the chapter. The philosophy behind the *I Ching* formed the basis of Taoism; therefore, one way of seeing how the authors of the book explained its working as an oracle (a means of foretelling the future) is to review the principles of Taoism.

Taoists believe that everything in the universe comes from an eternal, absolute source which they call T'ai Chi. Everything in our world originates from T'ai Chi and eventually flows back to it; in a sense, therefore, it controls all the changes which occur in our lives. Change can be of two sorts: cyclical, like the changes of the seasons, the ebb and flow of the tides, the waxing and waning of the moon, and such like; and sequential, as when our lives change as a consequence of our decisions and actions. Although change never ceases, it is not random or chaotic: it acts in accordance with a set of laws. For the cyclical changes, these laws are clear enough. The phases of the moon, for example, can be calculated in advance if we know the laws by which the planets revolve around the solar system. But sequential change is more difficult to define by a set of rules. We would all like to believe that each event in our life is an effect, and that we have control of the causes by our decisions and actions. The philosophy behind the *I Ching* suggests that it is impossible to gain total control of our lives, because what appear to be sequential changes are in fact only parts of very complicated cycles. The following analogy may help the reader to understand this.

We picture the changes in our lives as cause and effect – a straight line, as it were. Taoists picture change in our lives as a series of cycles – interweaving circles. Yet these two apparently different views may in reality not be so very different after all, for physics tells us that a straight line is really a circle of infinite diameter. Thus both Taoist and Western viewpoints encompass different parts of the same truth. The purpose of using the *I Ching* is to gain insight into how these cycles will affect our lives. By doing so, we can ensure that whatever we have in mind is carried out at the best time and in the way which accords best with prevailing cycles of change. People who are able to do this will not struggle fruitlessly against the course of events and thereby save themselves from needless pain, frustration and disappointment. This, then, is the first function of the *Book of Change:* to give advice on how we can assist our lives by following the cycles of cosmic law and order. Clearly, the advantages of choosing the correct course of action when faced with an important decision may be considerable. John Blofeld illustrates the point by analogy when he writes:

> Though we cannot, by holding up our hand and using Words of Power, bid the wind and waves to cease, we can learn to navigate the treacherous currents by conducting ourselves in harmony with the prevailing processes of transformation; thus we can safely weather successive storms in this life . . .[1]

The course of action, or 'way', that is currently in harmony with the forces of change is the *Tao*. At any moment, at least in theory, an infinitely large number of ways is available to each one of us. And the future may hold very different fortunes for us, depending on which of these ways we choose to take. The *Book of Change* can guide us towards the one which will be of most benefit to us, and let us foresee the consequences of other courses of action. (We shall see how this is done in a moment.) But it would be wrong to think that the Book can only reveal details of your own personal future. Far from it. The use of the Book as an oracle or divination system extends to any matter relating to any person, place, object or time. The one condition needed for success is that the enquirer should approach his task with the right attitude of mind – a point to which we shall return later.

How is it that the *I Ching* can reveal details of events that have not yet happened? Once again, the Taoist viewpoint is helpful in approaching the solution to this question. Taoist philosophy may or may not be correct, but it is one of the main traditions associated with the *I Ching* in its present form. To have knowledge of a system so closely related to the *I Ching* can only be of benefit to the man or woman who approaches it with an enquiry. What follows is a simplified presentation of Taoism as I understand it.

The cycles of change controlling all events in the universe depend upon T'ai Chi (the Absolute). T'ai Chi itself is said to be composed of two complementary forces called 'Yang' and 'Yin'; these enter all creation and give it form. The Yang and Yin content of any entity may fluctuate, and so, in turn, the nature of an object or individual and its position in relation to the future also changes. Yang and Yin, incidentally, are not 'good' and 'evil'. Neither is better or worse than the other. They are simply a necessary part of everything in existence. The *I Ching* allows us to discover the balance of Yang and Yin forces operating in either our lives or any other subject about which we make an enquiry. It also predicts how these forces will change, and thereby gives us insight into how we can work with them to achieve the best possible results. (I shall offer explanations of the *I Ching's* action in a non-Taoist framework later in the chapter.)

In its original form, the Book offered only two answers to questions put to it: 'yes' and 'no'. These alternatives were represented by Yang and Yin respectively. Yang is symbolized by a line thus: — and Yin by a line thus: -- . Clearly, the usefulness of the *I Ching* as an oracle was limited by the choice of only two answers. Fortunately over a period of time it was developed into a more sophisticated system of divination. The first step was to extend the meanings of the Yang and Yin lines, thus:[2] Yang (—) heaven, positive, masculine, active, strong; Yin (--) earth, negative, feminine, passive, yielding. Tradition has it that Emperor Fu Hsi developed eight trigrams, that is, combinations of three Yang and/or Yin lines, to which he ascribed meaning by divine inspiration. The eight trigrams are:

≡   Ch'ien; heaven, creative, active, father

☷ K'un; earth, receptive, passive, mother
☳ Chen; thunder, arousing, eldest son
☴ Sun; wind, gentle, eldest daughter
☵ K'an; water, dangerous, second son
☲ Li; fire, clinging, second daughter
☶ Ken; mountain, immovable, youngest son
☱ Tui; lake, joyful, youngest daughter.

The trigrams ☰ and ☷ represent Yang and Yin in pure form. For this reason, they are called the father and mother of the other six trigrams. King Wen, who lived around 1150 BC, later extended still further the number of possible responses, by combining the eight trigrams in all possible pairs to produce sixty-four hexagrams. By a process of deduction, we can see how he worked out logical meanings for each pair of trigrams. For example, Hexagram Eleven, T'ai, Peace, ䷊ represents an interaction of heaven ☰ and earth ☷ so complete that heaven is actually supporting earth. To obtain this hexagram in response to an enquiry would, naturally, be very favourable; it implies that one's actions are in accordance with the current cycles of change (or heaven's will, if you prefer). On the other hand, Hexagram Twelve, P'i, Stagnation ䷋ is not favourable because the intercourse of heaven and earth so necessary for success in our earthly activities is not taking place.

Guidance and advice about *any* relationships, events and situations can be obtained from the hexagrams. To take but one example, a hexagram containing the K'an trigram twice ䷜ implies great danger: K'an itself means danger, and repeated twice, the message is amplified. The multiple meanings ascribed to the trigrams give a variety of possible meanings to the hexagrams. This is why the answers of the oracle should be interpreted in the light of each enquiry.

As I suggested above, Yang and Yin are constantly fluctuating in accordance with the prevailing cycles of change. Suppose one asks a question of the *I Ching* which requires an answer in two parts: the first relevant to the present, and the second relevant to the future. The corresponding variations in Yang and Yin are reflected in the lines of the hexagram obtained during your consultation of the oracle. A line which is about to change into its opposite – thereby reflecting a variation in the Yang/Yin balance of your situation – is called a 'moving line'. Moving Yang lines are represented thus: ——o—— and moving Yin lines thus: —x—. Such lines extend the usefulness of the *I Ching* considerably. First, the *I Ching* offers a special explanation for each moving line in a hexagram. Also, after interpreting the hexagram in the normal way, one redraws it with each of the moving lines changed into its opposite: Yang to Yin, and vice versa. The second hexagram thus formed is said to represent matters concerning your enquiry at a point further into the future. Readers with mathematical ability will be able to work out the number of possible answers, excluding the moving lines themselves, which the *I Ching* can provide in response to an enquiry. There are sixty-four hexagrams; any line or lines in a hexagram may be moving lines. Thus we have sixty-three possibilities afterwards. This gives a total of 4032 possible responses to each question.

At this point, we should move on to consider the method of divination itself. The basis of all divination systems is some form of mechanical manipulation of objects. The pattern which emerges amongst the objects during this process is then 'translated' into language by looking it up in a code of reference. Obviously, in the case of the *I Ching*, this code of reference is the text of the sixty-four hexagrams. How, then, does one obtain a hexagram in response to an enquiry? There are two methods, one of which is vastly more complicated than the other. The more complex one is revered by many mystics and students of the *I Ching*. How far this is due to their desire to preserve an aura of mystery around the Book, it is impossible to say.

The simpler method involves tossing three coins into the air from the cupped hands, and noting which way they fall. In ancient China a particular type of Chinese coin was used; we dispense with such formality and use any three coins of the same denomination and year. The side of the coins detailing their monetary value corresponds to the inscribed side of the Chinese coin. This side is given a value of two. The reverse side, which corresponds to 'heads', is given a value of three. The coins are tossed onto the floor or a table surface. The combination of inscribed and reverse sides so obtained is totted up using the values of two for the inscribed side and three for the reverse:

- Three inscribed sides equals a value of 6, which is the Ritual Number of a moving Yin line —x—
- Two inscribed and one reverse side equals 7, which is the Ritual Number of a Yang line ———

- Two reverse and one inscribed side equals 8, which is the Ritual Number of a Yin line — —
- Three reverse sides equals 9, which is the Ritual Number of a moving Yang line—o—

The first line obtained by throwing the three coins is the bottom line of the hexagram. The process is then repeated to obtain the second line, that is, the next line upwards, and so on, until the top, sixth, line has been obtained from the sixth throw of the three coins. During this procedure the question to which an answer is required is held in the mind. I have dealt at some length with the formation of the hexagram by coin tossing at this point because I wish to discuss the implications of the method.

First of all, let me make it clear that the *I Ching* is not our only means of foretelling the future. It is possible to use a straightforward procedure rather like psychometry, which consists of relaxing into alpha and turning your mind to a question about the future. You simply note the impressions which then come to mind. Alternatively, after establishing a suitable code for 'yes/no', or 'favourable/unfavourable', or 'good/bad', one could put questions about the future to the dowsing pendulum. But we know, or at least can guess, how these techniques work. If the forces of Yang and Yin do not actually exist, as I believe, then why do the coins fall in such a way as to indicate which particular hexagram and moving lines refer to an enquiry? The simplest, and least adequate, explanation is that subconsciously controlled muscle movements make the coins fall in a particular pattern. This cannot, in fact, be correct. First, the divination system works even if you keep your eyes shut while tossing the coins. Second, the coins may leave your hands with heads or tails uppermost, but they frequently turn when they hit the ground.

C.G. Jung tried to explain divination by reference to his concept of synchronicity. This concept suggests that my throw of the coins at any moment in time is connected with all the other events occurring in the universe at that particular moment. Because of this peculiar interdependence of events, the fall of the coins mirrors the matter I have in mind. Such an explanation is far from adequate; not least because of one particular practical consideration. Suppose I throw the coins and ask a question about the prosperity of Britain in the year 1990. It can make no difference to the answer whether I ask this question in 1960 or

1980. But the universal situation at those two times may very well be quite different.[3]

So it appears that we must apply some reasoning to the problem. This is how I see the situation: (1) the relationship of the coins to the hexagrams is fixed; (2) generally only one hexagram is a relevant answer to your enquiry; (3) presumably you do not know what the answer is, or you would not be asking the question; (4) the conclusion derived from these three facts is that your mind must be doing two things during an enquiry. It must first of all work out the answer in a way which corresponds with the way in which it picks up information during precognition. And thereafter it must ensure the coins fall in such a way that they indicate the correct answer. Presumably this could be a psychokinetic process. An alternative explanation is that the subconscious simply knows when to release the coins so that they fall in the pattern necessary to produce the required answer. Clearly there will be several moments during the period in which you are throwing the coins when they would fall correctly. At first sight it is difficult to accept this explanation for the reason given above, that is, the coins may turn after they have left your hands or when they hit the surface. But it is possible to extend the argument and suggest that the subconscious knows this, too. Indeed, there is actually some evidence to suggest that both this process *and* psychokinesis play a part in controlling the fall of the coins.

Divination is an especially effective psychic technique. Indeed, in terms of the success rate for those who have no previous psychic experience, it ranks alongside dowsing. The reason for this is not hard to find. The use of a tool (dowsing pendulum or three coins with the *I Ching*) allows the subconscious mind to express information directly. In other words, the activity of the conscious mind is avoided during the reception of information. Compare this with telepathy, psychic healing (Chapter 12) and psychometry. These are techniques where the conscious mind, with all its critical judgements and irrelevant thoughts, is an essential part of the procedure! But let us now turn to some other points raised by the use of the *I Ching*.

Generally speaking, our patterns of behaviour, thoughts, feelings and emotions are fairly well defined; that is, predictable. All of us, if we are honest, must admit that. So it is quite likely that an outside observer who knows you well enough could predict what you are likely to do in certain sorts of situation.

Presumably, if an outside observer can do this, so too can your own subconscious. This implies that any question which involves psychological insights into your own consciousness can be answered directly from your own mind. When the *I Ching* is consulted on such matters, it is most likely that your subconscious causes the coins to fall in a way that leads to an appropriate hexagram. Whether or not you have read the *I Ching* is irrelevant, because you have a clairvoyant faculty which can provide knowledge of what is written in the texts.

Such reasoning suggests that the *I Ching* has a second major use: it allows one to gain insight into one's own psyche. Sometimes it forces us to recognize something in our minds which we may have been unwilling to admit to ourselves. Sometimes it tells us what we could have worked out for ourselves if we had been prepared to do so. And sometimes it merely confirms what is already in our minds. This last point is very important, and needs to be considered at greater length. Suppose that you had already decided on a particular course of action, but you were not prepared to admit the fact. You might consult the *I Ching*, ostensibly to ask what would be the best course of action in view of the alternatives open to you. Your real motivation, however, would be the hope of obtaining confirmation that your decision was correct. It would not be surprising if you did indeed receive an answer which confirmed the wisdom of what you had already decided to do! You must approach the *I Ching* with a willingness to accept answers which may not be what you consciously wish to be told. We shall return to this point later.

One question which repeatedly crops up when people use systems of divination is that of free will. How, they ask, can we be considered creatures with free will – the power to make independent, autonomous choices – if we are able to foretell the future in a way which suggests that our lives are set upon predetermined pathways? I will consider this question from a theoretical philosophical viewpoint, and then compare my conclusions with what I have written about Taoist philosophy. Strangely enough, the question of whether man has free will is not really very important to the use of the *I Ching*. To understand this view, we must develop an argument which rests on one basic assumption: the answers given by the *I Ching* to a person who consults it in the correct frame of mind are *never wrong*. (This excludes the special case mentioned earlier, that is, when we come to the *I Ching* determined to have it substantiate a viewpoint which we already hold.) Difficulties in interpretation may occur, certainly, but the answers always turn out to be correct in the light of future events. Suppose you wished to obtain information about the future state of affairs related to some particular matter at a specific point in time. This kind of enquiry is an absolute – that is, there is only one possible answer. From our viewpoint in the present, it often seems that there are many possible states of affairs for any point in the future. And this is indeed correct. But there can only be one state actually manifested at a certain point in the future. It is that state which you are asking about. An example should help to make this clear.

You might consult the oracle to discover whether or not you will be married five years from today. The *I Ching* will provide you – assuming your mind is open to receive any answer – with a true statement; in this case, basically 'yes' or 'no'. And five years from now, this statement will be seen to be true – you will either be married or you will not. But if the statement is true at that point in time, then obviously it must always have been true in the past, be true now, and will always be true in the future. Now, philosophers tell us that if a statement is true prior to the event it describes, it is impossible for that event not to happen. In other words, our lives would seem to be mapped out or pre-determined. This point of view, which is called 'determinism', rests upon the belief that every event in the universe is the inevitable outcome of previous events. Thus, for example, as I write these words, I do not do so from free choice; in fact I could not possibly write anything else, because each word is the inevitable result of all previous sensory input to my brain, all my previous thoughts and deliberations, all my previous experience and all my memories.

This conclusion may be unpleasant and difficult to accept. One's initial reaction runs something like this: 'Surely it cannot be that all my hopes and desires, beliefs and actions, thoughts and feelings, talents and abilities, character and personality, are nothing more than the reducible outcome of my previous experience?'

Let us examine the opposite side of the argument. The most obvious reason for believing that free will *does* exist is that all (or at any rate most) of us are convinced we are in control of our actions. But consider a man under hypnosis, who is instructed to perform a certain action when he is 'awakened'. He might be told to 'open the door when anyone mentions "elephants"'. And when that word is mentioned in subsequent conversation, the subject does indeed get up and open the door. Ask him why and he might say something like: 'It's too hot in here.' Further, he is convinced that the action was of his own volition, and it is impossible to persuade him otherwise. Clearly, though, the action was not of his own choosing. Equally clearly, this line of argument is not sound enough to support the idea of free will.

A similar refutation can be applied to the suggestion that our actions must be free because we base them upon relevant deliberation or claim that we are responsible for the consequences of our decisions. Determinism, if true, applies to everything. Deliberating before reaching a decision and feeling responsible for what has happened, therefore, would also be nothing more than events that are the inevitable outcome of previous causes.

The complete cases for and against free will and determinism are too complicated to present here. Suffice it to say that neither viewpoint can be proven or disproven conclusively. There are references to other works on the subject in the notes at the end of the chapter.[4] But how does this debate relate to our use of the *I Ching*? First of all, it may have occurred to you that the example given above – 'Will I be married in five years' time?' – is logically inconsistent with the proposal that the *I Ching*'s answers to such questions are true and therefore inevitable.For, as a result of such a prediction, you might change your behaviour and thereby make the prediction false. Simplistically, a determinist would say that such a change in your behaviour was itself a necessary part of the sequence of events leading up to the fulfilment of the prediction. A more sophisticated way of avoiding this logical difficulty is to assume that any predictions are made in such a way that they take account of the reaction of the subject being told them. A logician can show that this is theoretically possible, and so we are forced to admit that this particular difficulty is removed; and, as a consequence, that the *I Ching* could equally well answer all the types of question which I have mentioned so far, whether or not our behaviour was free or determined.

But let us consider another type of question which one might wish to put to the oracle. Suppose you are faced with one of the many choices which confront all of us from time to time: to take a new job, or not; to end a relationship, or not; to take a holiday in one place or another; to sign a deal, or to try for better terms; and so on and so on. In this type of situation (that is, where a choice must be made from one or more alternatives) the *I Ching* must be used as an oracle with a great deal of care. The language of the texts makes it inaccessible to questions of an either/or nature such as: 'Should I take the job at Brown's or Smith's?' Although the answer to this question would be correct, it would probably be impossible to understand. Instead, two questions should be presented: 'What would be the likely outcome if I accepted the job at Brown's?' and, 'What would be the likely outcome if I accepted the job at Smith's?' The final decision would be based on a consideration of the hexagrams received in answer to each question.

Suppose that, in such a 'choice situation', you had asked appropriate questions and received replies which clearly indicated that one option was likely to be much more favourable than the other(s). Presumably you could either accept or reject that advice. If you *accept* it, a free-will supporter would say that you chose to do so. A determinist would say that your decision to accept it was inevitable, that all your previous thoughts and so on had led you to a point where the *I Ching*'s advice simply tipped you onto a particular path of action. Yet both these arguments are equally valid if you *reject* the advice of the *I Ching*! Clearly, such reasoning is futile. Let us try to resolve the free will/determinist debate in a different way.

In a 'choice situation', the *I Ching* makes a prediction about the possible outcomes of a variety of different courses of action. This can only be done with a knowledge of all the factors, both human and environmental, which would come into play if each situation were to be realized. (For the moment, we are not concerned with who or what has this knowledge or, more accurately, information.) To say that the *I Ching* can predict one's future in this way is equivalent to suggesting that the 'force' behind the *I Ching* has access to well-defined information: access not only to information about one's present position in the world, but also to information about all the factors which might influence that position so as to produce your specific position at any point in the future. Now, compare that last statement with the following expression of determinist philosophy: 'If the present condition of a system and the laws governing its behaviour are both known completely, the state of that system at any point in the future can be determined.' Clearly, my suggestions about the *I Ching* are very similar to statements which summarize determinist philosophy. The obvious conclusion is that prediction equals determinism.

This conclusion was also implicit in my previous observations about the *I Ching's* answers to absolute questions. But is it correct? As you might expect by now, there is in fact an equally convincing line of reasoning which seems to prove that prediction does *not* imply determinism. As I understand it, this is because the very language used to describe a predicted event is incapable of defining that event in every detail. Of course, we can make descriptions more and more precise and less open to interpretation, but inevitably there is a point at which descriptions are simply unable to discriminate between two events which differ in minute detail. Yet to say that an event is determined is to claim that it is specifically defined by its characteristics. (Remember, the characteristic properties of each event are unique and derived from a set of laws governing every aspect of the behaviour of a system.) In other words, while deterministic theory claims that every event must be determinate, no prediction can identify a determinate event with certainty. Thus predictability and determinism are not equivalent notions. A prediction always describes a *class* of possible events – even though the differences between the events in that class may be beyond our ability to analyse them. This is actually just one of many arguments against the assertion that prediction equals determinism. To sum up, two things are clear: one, philosophical debate does not solve the problem of free will versus determinism; two, neither does a consideration of the practical use of the *I Ching*. But we have still one avenue to explore: the views of the ancient Chinese. How did they see the relationship between the future and the *I Ching*?

The ancient Chinese did not think of the future as an unchanging, determined progression of events. They regarded it as a series of changes acting in accordance with sets of laws. And using the *I Ching* allowed them to foresee the outcome of those laws at work. By doing so, they could choose their actions so that they acted in accordance with one or other cycle – hopefully, the one which was most favourable. The extent to which man can work against the cosmic cycles, they suggested, is limited: the will of heaven has always been too strong for the average man.

The use and interpretation of the *I Ching*

To Westerners, much of the Book's language seems strange. Constant references to the 'Superior Man', to 'winning advantage' and so on, all need explanation. But before we consider these points, let us turn our attention to wider aspects of the use of the *Book of Change*. Anybody who wishes to consult the *I Ching* must first obtain a copy of the texts of the hexagrams. There are several available: some of the more notable ones are listed in the notes at the end of the chapter.[5] I have already explained the method of divination using coins; full instructions for the alternative techniques should be included with any copy of the hexagram texts. Because divination is a psychic technique, it is helpful to be at alpha while using the *I Ching*. However, for the reason already explained (page 127), this is not essential Chinese scholars thought so much of the power of the *I Ching* that they treated each enquiry as a special consultation and used the Book only in unusual or difficult circumstances.[6] We do well to follow their example, but for different reasons. They regarded the book as a means of sampling Yang and Yin forces of immense power and therefore treated it rather as a sacred object. I regard it as a means of very effectively tapping into our psychic faculty, which is a normal part of our being. But superficial or improper use of the *I Ching* is less likely to produce a meaningful answer, a fact which, in turn, makes you less likely to approach the Book with the correct attitude of mind when you do need guidance. So what is the correct attitude? It has several distinct characteristics, which can be listed as follows:

(1)   You must have a genuine reason for consulting the *I Ching*: that is, the question you ask should have a real importance.

(2)   You must accept that the *I Ching* really can answer your question: you need not positively believe in it, but if you completely deny its power, you are unlikely to receive an answer to your enquiry.

(3)   You must ensure that your enquiry is exact and correctly constructed: either/or questions are especially unsuitable, and it is essential to specify the details to which your enquiry refers, for example, 'What will be the likely outcome for my financial situation within the next two years if I take the job I've been offered?'

(4)   You must be open to the possibility of receiving an answer

which you do not like: I have explained elsewhere how the *I Ching* can be influenced by anything which is already a certainty in your own mind.

Interpreting the hexagrams

When you have posed your question, obtained a hexagram, and re-drawn the moving lines (if any) to form a second hexagram, you are ready to look up the texts. Take great care not to make any mistakes when you do this, otherwise the whole exercise will be pointless.

Each hexagram is divided into several parts. The first part is called the *decision, text* or *judgement*. This was the work of King Wen and his son Duke Chou. The next part, the *commentary*, was added by Confucius. It was he who interpreted the form of the hexagrams and the interrelationships of the different lines. (Yang lines were held to represent objects or people who had a fund of active or creative power. Yin lines represented rather more passive qualities. But because both were essential elements of all existence, the exact meaning of the hexagram could only be derived from an analysis of the whole, rather than the individual lines.) The third part of the hexagram is called the *image* or *symbol*. It provides a pictorial representation of the hexagram and suggests how the Superior Man (see below) would act in the circumstances. Finally, there are the *moving lines*. They are composed of text written by Duke Chou and a translation into language appropriate to our existence. This translation is known as the *meaning*.

Some phrases occur many times in the hexagrams. For example, the *Superior Man* represents an ideal towards which we should all strive. His actions are all in accord with the prevailing Tao; he stands above human frailties. Since your aim is to select the correct Tao, you may take references to the Superior Man as indicative of what your behaviour would best be in the circumstances relating to your enquiry. Naturally, all the qualities of the enlightened or spiritually aware are possessed by the Supierior Man: spirituality as opposed to materialism, virtue, righteousness, wisdom, incorruptibility and such like. Although most of us cannot claim such qualities, the *I Ching* can show us how to increase the part they play in our lives.

The terms *great man* and *sage* represent, respectively, a man (or woman) who has authority or leadership and a man (or woman) who has considerable wisdom which can be applied to your situation. Such people will be in a position to assist with your enquiry. Unfortunately, their identities may not be very clear. If the matter seems important, you can always put further questions to the *I Ching*.

Crossing the great water represents an undertaking of importance. This phrase originated in times when crossing the Yangtze river was just such an undertaking. Nowadays we interpret this phrase to mean either 'taking a journey overseas' or 'overcoming some obstacle' or 'undertaking something of importance'.

Let us now consider some examples of the use of the *I Ching* and the interpretation of the hexagrams. In these examples,[7] and with your own experience of divination, you will notice that by no means all of the hexagram is actually relevant to the particular enquiry. (This is an inevitable feature of any system of divination which uses a written code.) Quite frequently, in fact, the moving lines are the clearest guide to an enquiry. On the first read-through of the hexagram, something may or may not strike you as being particularly obvious or relevant. If it does, you may have found the complete answer to your enquiry. If it does not, the answer may lie concealed within the language of the texts and commentaries. The correct way to approach such a situation is to read through the hexagram and consciously consider any possible meanings to what is written there. This transfers the information to your subconscious, the part of your mind which is most closely associated with the subtle psychological nuances of the *I Ching*. Thereafter, the real meaning of the text may dawn on you as a flash of insight. Interpretation is also assisted if you are in a quiet, contemplative frame of mind when you try to understand the answer to your enquiry. This emphasizes the role which intuition plays in our work with the *I Ching*.

Example A

Just before the 1979 general election was held in Britain, I thought that it would be interesting to find out about the result of the election. Accordingly I put the question, 'What will be the outcome of the next election?' to the *I Ching*. At the time of the election, the Labour party held office, and the Prime Minister was a man. Let us now see what answer I received to my question. The six lines made up the following hexagram: ☱

This is hexagram number 49, Ko, meaning 'Revolution' or 'Change'. The moving lines, when changed to their opposites, produce the following: ☷ , which is hexagram 44, Kou, meaning 'Contact'. The name of the first hexagram was obviously a clear indication that we could expect a change of government. And the Conservatives were indeed victorious on the day. In fact, their majority was much larger than had generally been expected. This is especially interesting in view of the following sentence in the text: 'Not before the day of its [i.e. revolution's] completion will men have faith in it.' As far as the moving lines are concerned, this seems to be a case where they had no directly relevant meaning of their own. For example, the text of line 2 reads: 'On the day the revolution is completed, to advance brings good fortune and is free from error.' Yet my enquiry had not asked if the time was favourable for a particular action. So I passed straight on to hexagram 44. (When you have received one or more moving lines, and therefore have a second hexagram to interpret, you only refer to the text, commentary and image of the second hexagram.) The text of this hexagram reads, in part, 'Women wield the power'. British readers will at once see the significance of that – in 1979 the leader of the Com- servative Party was a woman, for the first time ever, and it was she who became Prime Minister after the election! Interestingly, there is nothing else in hexagram 44 of any relevance. To sum up, the *I Ching* gave me two answers to the question I had asked of it: first, that the government would change, and second, that a woman would become PM. I suspect that if I had asked, 'Which party will win the next election?' I would not have received any reference to the second hexagram.

Example B
While I was writing this chapter, I decided to ask the *I Ching* a question on the subject uppermost in my mind: 'Will this book be useful to people who wish to develop their psychic ability?' In reply, I received one of the two most important hexagrams of the *I Ching*, number 2, K'un, The Passive Principle: ☷ This is remarkable. The probability of obtaining this hexagram with no moving lines *by chance alone* is only 1 in 4000. This strongly suggests that it was no fluke of the coin throwing which produced it. I was surprised because one rarely obtains a pure Yang or Yin hexagram. When one does so, it is an auspicious event: they are a powerful pair, hexagrams 1 and 2. But what does this mean in relation to my enquiry? In the text, we find 'Sublime success ... The Superior Man has an objective and

sets forth to gain it. At first he goes astray, but later finds his bearings.' This could refer to my initial doubts about exactly what contents should be included in this book. I presume that this book's contents are also the subject of the following sentence in the commentary: 'It is an all-embracing, shining vessel brimming with multitudinous contents.' [!] There is a strong suggestion that the book is in accord with the Passive Principle, the terrestial Yin forces, and because of this, 'becomes bright and shines forth'. (You do not need to believe in the concept of Yang and Yin to interpret the hexagrams: remember, you are looking for the sentences and expressions which seem most likely to 'contain' the answer to your enquiry.) In passing, we should note that answers like this one are sometimes a reflection of one's existing impressions or opinions. I offer no comments on whether or not that is true in this particular case!

Example C
A friend who had been reading about psychic work asked me why 'psychic techniques sometimes work, and sometimes don't'. I suggested that he consulted the *I Ching*. The answer to that question was hexagram 6, Sung, Conflict: ☰☵ Neither the text nor the commentary seemed particularly relevant, in my opinion. Indeed, all I could suggest was that 'conflict' might imply he had some personal conflict with the concept of psychic work which was hindering his success. However, he suggested that statements in the text, about danger and firmness meeting to produce conflict, related to some personal difficulties which were worrying him at the time. An alternative interpretation, which I thought more likely, could be derived from the wording of the image, or symbol: 'The Superior Man does not embark upon any affair until he has carefully planned the start.' This strongly suggests that a person of wisdom would not try to use psychic techniques unless he knew what he was going to do with them (both in the short and long term), and perhaps also unless he understood his real motivation for trying them.

Example D
Another person I know has some musical talent, and at one point had been idly considering whether to become a professional or semi-professional musician. Because she was so uncertain of what to do, I consulted the *I Ching* (without her knowledge) to try and obtain a clear perspective of the situation,

in the hope that any information I received would help her make a decision. The question was: 'Could Helen make a success of a professional or semi-professional musical career?' The coins fell in such a way as to produce hexagram 16, Yu, Repose, with moving lines at positions 2, 4 and 6: ䷏ The text of this hexagram reads: 'Repose profits those engaged in building up the country and sending forth armies.' Although that may seem irrelevant, John Blofeld informs us that it means 'perfect certainty as to the rightness of our cause is of great value under the conditions mentioned'. So Helen would obviously have to be completely sure of her decision before embarking on a musical career. However, the commentary on the text emphasizes that 'whatever is willed can be accomplished'; clearly a reminder that with determination one can achieve anything. There were one or two further hints to the same point in the commentary, but at first sight the symbol seemed meaningless: 'The ancient rulers venerated heaven's gifts with solemn music and they sacrificed abundantly to the Supreme Lord . . .' On reflection, however, I came to the conclusion that this meant music would be a worthwhile career for Helen. Maybe it even indicated the particular field in which she would be most successful (some field of religious music?) Enough speculation! Let us look at the moving lines. Number 2 refers to the mental repose which follows absolute confidence that a decision is correct; here, probably the decision to make music a career. It also makes the point that 'righteous persistence brings reward', suggesting ultimate success. Number 4 specifically advises that we should 'harbour no doubts', implying the decision is correct even if circumstances make it appear otherwise. And number 6 smartly rebukes anyone who wishes to do something but does not do it when the time is right: '[this line] implies being tardy to the point of extreme rashness in the face of . . . a need to act.' In other words, now is the time for the decision to be taken.

Hexagram 16 with these three moving lines becomes hexagram 4, Meng, Youthful Foolishness: ䷃ In the words of John Blofeld, this hexagram 'indicates a need for proper direction'. Now, remember that the second hexagram refers to events later in time than those described by the first hexagram. So it seemed very likely that if Helen did make a career in music, she would face the danger of going astray after some initial success in the field. Indeed, hexagram 4 is not very favourable. It hints of danger and failure through immaturity, lack of education or lack of firm aims. No doubt such problems could be overcome by careful planning. But how much more useful to be forewarned of possible problems than to know about them only when they have arrived!

That completes our review of divination. The next topic is an even more controversial and difficult one – psychic healing.

REFERENCES AND NOTES

1   J. Blofeld, *I Ching: The Book of Change* (Unwin paperbacks, London, 1976), p. 31.
2   For a full discussion of such matters, see any general reference work on the *I Ching* (e.g. Blofeld, op. cit.).
3   This point was made by Blofeld, op. cit., p. 25, although he used a different example.
4   See, for example, D. J. O'Connor, *Free Will* (Anchor Books, Doubleday, New York, 1971).
5   Three useful versions of the *I Ching* are:
    R. Wilhelm, *I Ching or Book of Changes* (Routledge and Kegan Paul, London, 1975); J. Blofeld, op. cit.; and A. Douglas, *The Oracle of Change: How to Consult the I Ching* (Penguin, London, 1972).
6   This point is emphasized by Blofeld, op. cit., p. 66.
7   I have used John Blofeld's translation in all the examples.

12.

Psychic Healing

Non-medical healing takes many forms. In this chapter we shall consider three of them: divine healing, spirit healing and psychic healing. I have included divine and spirit healing not because they are established techniques but because I intend to demonstrate that they are simply different names for the basic psychic healing process. Before reviewing the evidence which supports this line of reasoning, however, we should establish a clear picture of the belief systems which lie behind the different names.

Divine healing is perhaps best known as the healings which occasionally occur after prayers for the recovery of a sick person have been offered to God. Another form is the laying-on of hands practised by some priests in special healing services in church. In this procedure, the priest is supposedly a channel for the 'Power of God'. Thus, we can define a divine healing as any healing which is attributed to the intervention of God in human affairs.

There are those who maintain that God is 'above' events in the universe and therefore has no part in either causing, or curing, disease or illness. Such individuals may attribute supernormal healing to saints if they operate within an established religion or to discarnate spirits of dead human beings if they do not. (Supernormal healings are those which cannot be accounted for by either the normal action of the body's own healing system or medical intervention.)

The late Harry Edwards was probably Britain's best known spirit healer of recent years. His huge following and the many cures which he brought about suggest that we should examine his beliefs very carefully.[1] Edwards' philosophy was based on the belief that we have a spirit body and mind as well as a physical body and mind; the spirit body and mind pass on to the so-called astral plane when our physical existence on earth has ended. Edwards maintained that God is above all events in the universe and therefore cannot become involved in causing or curing illness. But no such limitations apply to spirits on the astral plane; they can, and do, intervene in human affairs, particularly in the field of healing. Spirits have more advanced knowledge and skills than we do, hence they can cure illness in a way which seems mysterious to us. But in order to heal they must be able to communicate with earth-bound humans. Just how do they do so?

Edwards repeatedly stated that the spirits can only communicate with the spirit mind of living people. Specifically, in fact, with the spirit mind of the healer. He acts as a link between the person being healed (the healee) and the spirit world in the following way: his spirit mind receives information from the spirit doctors. This information is then transmitted to the healer's consciousness – which is the overlapping of physical and spirit minds – and from there is passed to the 'bodily intelligence' of the healee. (The bodily intelligence is supposedly an organizing force of an unspecified nature which controls the distribution and organization of body chemicals and the organization of tissues and cells.) The healee's bodily intelligence uses the information provided in this way to correct any deficiency and thereby effect a cure. But some cures are so dramatic and rapid – almost instantaneous – that they cannot be explained in this way, and so it follows that the spirits must also be able to control some form of energy which can directly affect the structure of the human body. Just as the practitioners of divine healing have both a contact healing process (the laying-on of hands) and a distant healing technique (prayer), so too did Harry Edwards. During a contact healing, the healer is necessary to pass on the spirits' advice and assistance to the bodily intelligence of the subject. Presumably in a distant healing, the healer's role is limited to drawing the spirits' attention to the sick individual so that they can influence his or her bodily intelligence directly.

Reading Harry Edwards' books gives one the impression that he was attempting to explain his undoubted gifts by constructing a philosophy which he found personally acceptable and believable. To paraphrase one reviewer, it is a mixture of lay psychology, common sense and science of variable soundness. We can now see whether the techniques of psychic healers fall within a similar framework.

Psychic healers also heal either by physical contact with the sick subject or by a process of distant healing. And, rather like those who attribute supernormal healing to God or spirits, psychic healers do not believe that they are the source of the healing power. They talk instead of cosmic or psychic energy flowing through them. This may be a partial answer to the question of how contact healing actually works, but, as we shall see, it is probably a long way from the mark where distant healings are concerned. In general, however, most healers prefer to talk about techniques rather than offer explanations of how they achieve results.

Thelma Moss analysed the characteristics of several healers and discovered that they had a number of features in common.[2] This is our first evidence that 'divine', 'spirit' and 'psychic' healing are nothing more than different labels for the same basic procedure.

(1) *Genuine healers do not know how the healing process actually works.* This is summed up in a statement of Katherine Kuhlman, one of America's best known divine healers:

> Sometimes ... I stand there and see all these wonderful things happen and I don't understand *how* they happen or what happened to cause them to happen ...

We shall consider this point at greater length in a moment.

(2) *They are usually not taught to heal, but discover their ability for themselves.* Two of the United States' most famous healers were the late Ambrose Worrall and his wife Olga, who independently discovered their healing abilities before they met each other. Ambrose Worrall did not suspect he had the ability to heal until he was a young man. Then, one day, he felt an 'unknown power' impel him to place his hands on his sister's neck, which was paralysed after an accident. She was instantly cured. Olga Worrall, on the other hand, knew of her ability from childhood: she frequently alleviated pains and aches for her mother and other people by placing her hands on the painful area. Stories like these are commonplace amongst healers.

(3) *They do not claim that the ability to heal is their own.* This has, of course, already become clear from our review of healing.

(4) *They do not heal everyone.* Despite the fact that many healers have claimed almost a 100 per cent success rate in healing, there is no doubt that in reality a significant number of healings actually fail, and that in many cases the healee relapses after a short period of improvement. It is possible to analyse qualitatively the results of various healings. Sometimes a healee receives no physical benefit, but feels psychologically calm and peaceful. Sometimes physical improvements occur without any change in the psychology of the patient; these may be temporary or permanent, dramatic or moderate (a point which we shall discuss at length later). Sometimes psychological and physical changes of a long-lasting nature take place in the healee.

To this list, we can obviously add the observation that all healers use either contact or distant healing. The comparison between different types of healing can be extended by analysing healers' accounts of their experiences while healing and the similarities in their healing techniques. Lawrence LeShan has done just that. Before we examine his work, however, there is another important point to consider.

In the majority of supernormal healings, there is no medical evidence for any improvement in the subject's condition. This is because it is not available. The medical profession is made up of men and women who are dedicated to curing illness by well known scientific procedures. They are scornful of the possibility of any form of supernormal healing, and so do not regard it as something which they need to explain or co-operate with. This hostility has made it very difficult to obtain objective evidence for or against the reality of psychic healing. In fact, the problem is worse than that, because no genuine psychic healer would suggest that a healee foregoes medical advice. So a sick individual who turns to a psychic healer has nearly always been receiving medical care. Even if his or her recovery only begins when psychic healing is administered, who could say that the medical help was not responsible? Sometimes there are psychic cures which verge on the miraculous. In such cases, medical authorities generally offer one of two explanations: either that spontaneous remission has taken place, or that the patient has been cured through faith.

Spontaneous remissions do occur in cases where no form of non-medical healing has been applied and where the medical profession itself has given up all hope of recovery for the patient. There is no way of explaining how or why these spontaneous remissions occur in some cases and not others, but faith probably plays a part. This is not, of course, faith in a religious sense, but faith in the sense of an unshakeable belief; a belief, for example, that healing will occur naturally, or that doctors can cure any illness, or that psychic healers have a real and mysterious power.

This last statement may seem to suggest that the reality of psychic healing can never be 100 per cent proven. Such is not the case! First, we know that distant healing can be effective even when the healee is unaware that it is being applied. More importantly, however, there have been several objective scientific experiments which conclusively prove the reality of psychic healing. I shall describe these after we have considered the work of Lawrence LeShan.

LeShan analysed many healers' accounts of their techniques in an attempt to discover the 'secrets' of the healing process. He dismissed idiosyncratic behaviours or techniques, assuming, quite rightly in my opinion, that these were irrelevant to the healing process. His initial work seemed to confirm that the most obvious way of dividing all supernormal healing into different categories was to classify it as contact or distant healing.[3] Let us therefore examine some specific cases of contact and distant healing, beginning with three examples of contact healing. The first case is from a Christian healer's account of his work.

> ... we prayed together, and I gave the laying-on of hands. Some days later, when he made his visit, the doctor noticed that the reflexes in one of her legs, till then non-existent, began to manifest themselves afresh. Pastoral care lasted for five months. Towards the end, the patient ... put her life entirely into the hands of God, in order that He should do with her what He would. Three days later, she walked on her own in the corridors of the hospital. She had broken her backbone three years previously (through a fall downstairs) and for two years she had been completely paralysed. This cure has now lasted for three years.[4]

The next is from Harry Edwards' account of his spiritual healing:

> Mr Olsen had a 'spinal collapse'. After weeks of hospitalization he was worse and declared incurable. He had received all the usual hospital treatments. Finally ... he was encased in plaster from his neck to his thighs and sent home to endure his suffering. He was told he could have an unlimited number of pain-killing tablets. He

could not eat or sleep and signs of paralysis were setting in. [Eventually his wife and son cut the plaster off and took him to see Edwards.] Within five minutes, the back was adjusted and free mobility restored. He could walk easily and had no pain whatsoever ... Mr Olsen has not had a twinge of pain since and has driven his car many thousands of miles.[5]

And the third is from Lawrence LeShan's own experience of psychic healing:

A woman known to me ... had intermittent, very large 'cold sores' for over twenty years. Two or three times a year she would get one on her lip and it would take approximately thirty days to heal ... I held one hand on each side of her face, not touching the affected area, for about twenty minutes. Afterwards she reported that during the twenty minutes she had been conscious of several periods of heat, and one of 'tingling' in the lip area. About one half hour later she left my office to drive home (a drive of about an hour); en route she felt suddenly a strong 'tingling' in the lip area, she looked at it in the rear-view mirror, and in her words, 'I nearly had an accident I was so surprised. I pulled off the road and sat for ten minutes watching the new skin regrow. The dead skin in the centre did not seem to change, but new skin slowly grew over the whole raw pink area.' When she arrived home, her son and her husband both reacted in surprise to the complete unexpected change and almost complete healing of the cold sore. The next day it had returned about one-third the size it had been when she arrived in my office the day before, and disappeared over the next week.[6]

It would be wrong to assume that all healings of this sort are so dramatic. Many fail. Many produce only temporary improvement. Yet the number of successful cases reported is so large that one is certain something remarkable is happening. And the same is true of distant healing. The first example of distant healing which I have included was reported by Harry Edwards. It concerns a girl who was suffering from polio at such an advanced state that she had been put on a life-support machine: 'Medical opinion was that she could not live for more than three hours ... paralysis had affected the neck, brain [sic] and top half of the body. The heart beats were becoming fainter and slower. The left lung had stopped operating altogether.' Edwards applied distant healing at the request of the girl's parents. He reported: 'The doctors attending her could not understand how it was that she lived through the night and the next day.' Over the next six days, we are told, the girl gradually recovered the ability to breathe. Three weeks later, her voice returned and she began to take food. The doctors said that 'her recovery was not due to their efforts'. Healing was administered over a period of three months, and the girl recovered completely.[7]

The second case was reported by Lawrence LeShan. It concerns a fifteen-year-old boy who had broken his back on a trampoline. This boy was in a serious state: he had no feeling below his chest and only limited movement in his arm muscles; his legs and feet were completely senseless and paralysed. The healing was conducted by a group of students working with LeShan; the boy, Christopher, was unaware of what they were doing.

> On Sunday, between 11:55 and 12:15 in the day ... the group really 'turned on' in a very strong long-distance healing. In the early afternoon, Christopher suddenly called out that he could 'feel' his legs. It soon became apparent that he could not only feel pressure sensations, but 'could even tell which of his toes was being touched at any given time'. The father said ... 'that there is no explanation for this since the period of detraumatization was well over and no hope was held for any further improvement or restoration in Chris's physical condition'.[8]

At first sight, these cases do indeed seem to confirm the validity of a division of healing into the two categories of 'contact' and 'distant'. However, when one looks at healing from the viewpoint of the results, rather than the method, a quite different division becomes clear: there are healings which can be explained by the action of the body's natural healing system, albeit greatly accelerated; and there are healings which verge on the miraculous. (These are ones in which dramatic changes in body structure or function take place in a very short space of time.) Because I consider this division to be at least as important as the contact/distant one, I shall now explain it in more detail.

The majority of successful healings produce a recovery which seems to involve the body's natural healing system. Sometimes this is dramatically speeded up, but the basic series of events involved in a normal recovery is still obvious. This was noticed by Alexis Carrel, when he observed under a lens what happened to an open, visible cancer during a healing:[9]

> The cancer followed the usual, well known course a cancer follows when it regresses. These [sic] include specific courses of development in the formation of scar tissue fibres, changes in blood distribution, etc. This cancer, said Carrel, followed this progression,

but many many times faster than he had ever seen or heard of it happening before.

LeShan contrasts this with those rare healings which verge on the 'miraculous'. Consider the following healing by Rebecca Beard:

> In this case, a thirty-eight pound ascites tumour (a liquid tumour) disappeared overnight. During the night the healee did not get out of bed and the bed was not wet. It is hard to imagine the body having the ability to dispose of approximately thirty-eight pints of liquid in this way.[10]

Many other accounts show that this second type of healing is 'rare but real': examples include the manipulation and immediate free movement of joints which have been seized for years with deposits of calcium within the joint. Another predominant example of this rare type of healing includes the dispersal of tumours under the fingers of the healer while he works. The Worralls have written: 'Miraculous, instantaneous healings seldom occur, but we have had tumours and malignant growths shrivel up and disappear beneath our hands.'[11] All these observations led LeShan to formulate a three-fold classification of psychic healing, which I have modified slightly to fit within the framework of this book:

Type A (which LeShan termed type 2): the basic contact healing

Type B (which LeShan termed type 1): the distant healing technique which leads to progressive recovery at a rate anywhere between that of the normal healing process and a greatly accelerated one

Type C (which LeShan termed type 5): the 'miraculous' healings which are quite unlike normal recovery or healing.

I should point out that 'distant' does not necessarily imply healer and healee being miles apart. They may be together in the same room. And they may even be involved in a type A contact healing when the mechanism of a type B or C begins to operate. If this is so, you might wonder how one can differentiate between type A and type B/C. In fact the subjective nature of the experience clearly identifies the type of healing taking place. In a sense, type A healing is more like a physical process than type B/C. I shall now discuss these different types of healing in more detail and try to explain what is happening in each case.

The mechanism of healing

There is no doubt that all three types of healing involve altered states of consciousness. The healer's attention is not directed towards either himself or the physical world, yet neither is it turned inwards in self-contemplation. Perhaps the best description is that it is 'suspended', while awareness is maintained. This corresponds, of course, to the alpha level of mind described so many times in this book. The actual method which a healer uses to attain this altered state of consciousness depends upon both the framework within which he operates and his own personal beliefs. Some healers pray, some try to adopt a different way of looking at the world (to paraphrase LeShan), some relax and meditate, and others simply cannot explain it. The system used in this book is, as you are aware, relaxation and visualization. But before considering this, we need to know what healers actually *do* once they have reached the correct level of mind.

Type A healing

The most obvious feature of type A healing is that it involves physical contact, or at least a very close association, between healer and healee. While at the correct level of mind, the healer holds his hands on each side of the injured area. He might picture a white healing energy flowing down his right arm, through the patient and up his left arm. He might direct his attention to his fingers, as did Harry Edwards: 'The healer's whole being is concentrated on his fingers – nothing else seems to exist. The desired result is the only thing that is his concern.'[12] Or he might simply wait for the healing to happen. But despite these differences, in all cases the healer perceives a flow of energy or a vibration passing through him. In about 50 per cent of such cases, according to LeShan, the healee feels heat; 10 per cent feel 'activity', and a few report cold. Interestingly, these sensations are felt only when there *is* a physical problem – holding the hands on either side of healthy tissue produces no reaction at all.[13]

One striking feature of this contact, or 'laying-on of hands', is that it can calm emotionally troubled individuals as well as speeding the healing of physical injury. Unfortunately, however, the process drains both the physical and mental energy of the healer. The most reasonable conclusion which can be drawn from these observations is that the healer himself acts as the source of some form of healing energy during a type A healing. (We shall return to this point in the final chapter.) However, this draining effect does not occur if a 'mixed' type A/B or A/C healing takes place; therefore the method of contact healing described at the end of this chapter is designed towards that end.

Scientific tests on contact healing

There have been very few scientific tests conducted on the healing process. To date, the best demonstration that contact healing really does affect the healee is a series of experiments conducted on one Oskar Estebany by Dr Bernard Grad of McGill University in Canada.[14] Estebany was a former Hungarian cavalry officer who first became aware of his healing ability when he noticed the way in which nervous horses calmed down when he was near them. But his healing abilities were frowned upon by the Hungarian authorities, and he emigrated to Canada in 1956. Shortly afterwards, he met Dr Grad, who was so impressed by Estebany that he decided to conduct the experiments described here.

Grad deliberately removed measured areas of skin from the backs of three hundred mice. These were then divided into three groups: the first group received no handling at all, the second was handled by Estebany, and the third was handled by medical students who did not claim to have supernormal healing ability. Handling consisted of simply holding the mice's cages for twenty minutes each day. To ensure that the different groups of mice were equal in all other respects, the laboratory assistants who fed and cleaned the animals were not told which group was which. The experiment produced some remarkable results. After only fourteen days of the eighteen-day experimental period, the mice handled by Estebany were almost completely wound-free. There was no significant difference between the other two groups, both of which still showed large areas of injury. Thus the animals handled by Estebany had healed much more quickly than those in the other two groups.

An even more fascinating result was obtained in an experiment with germinating barley seeds.[15] Dr Grad heated the seeds to a point where they were damaged but not killed. He then divided them at random into two groups and planted them under identical conditions of humidity, soil and light. One group was subsequently watered with untreated solution of the type used for human intravenous infusions; the other group received a similar solution after it had been held by Estebany for thirty minutes. He did not touch the seeds themselves. Once again, the results were astonishing. The seeds which received the treated water showed a higher rate of germination, and subsequently grew more quickly.

Unlike many experiments in this field, Grad's were beyond reproach. But, more importantly, they were the first objective proof that healers do affect living material in some way. Of course, the experiments described above do not tell us how healers affect living tissue. It was Dr Sister Justa Smith of Rosary Hill College, New York, who provided information on that question. She reasoned that Estebany might be affecting the action of enzymes in the tissues which he healed. (Enzymes are catalysts which regulate the chemical reactions of every cell in every living organism.) She invited Estebany along to her laboratory, where she discovered that he was indeed able to alter the structure of enzymes in such a way that their activity increased.[16] You will observe that a speeding up of chemical reactions in the cells of the body could exactly account for the acceleration of the body's healing system which is seen in type A and B healing. Other scientists have conducted investigations which suggest that some form of energy emanates from the healer's hands. It has been shown that the molecular structure of water is slightly modified (the angle between the hydrogen and oxygen atoms increases slightly) when a healer brings his hands near it. However, this is not to say that a psychic healer alters the molecular structure of water in the healee's body. Rather, we might conclude that healers have the ability to control some form of energy; an energy which can modify the rate of chemical reactions and the structure of chemical compounds in the body of the healee. For want of a better expression, let us call this 'psychic energy'.

It appears that type A contact healings tend to have transient results. This fits in with the suggestion made earlier that, in contact healing, the healer is himself the source of the healing energy: just as we have only so much physical energy, presumably we have only a certain amount of psychic energy, which can be drained away during the contact healing procedure. As a kind of coincidental confirmation of this idea, it is noticeable that the most famous – and presumably successful – healers all produce the more powerful and effective types B and (rarely) C.

Types B and C healing

To recap, types B and C appear to involve two distinct processes: B involves an acceleration of the body's healing system, while type C verges on the 'miraculous'. LeShan has suggested that the accelerated rate of body change which occurs during and after a type B healing represents the full potential of the body which is normally never achieved.[17] This is an interesting suggestion. It implies that our thinking is inverted: 'normal' healing is in fact the abnormal process, and psychic healing merely allows us to reach what is our natural potential. There is, however, no easy way of explaining type C healings. (We must keep an open mind about the possibility that type B and C healings are actually opposite ends of a spectrum, and that any intermediate degree of healing is possible. This might explain why so few healers have ever explicitly distinguished between the different types.)

As in the case of type A healings, the healer starts the process by altering his level of consciousness. Once he has done this, however, the procedure is noticeably different to the type A procedure. For one thing, these healings do not 'just happen': a positive thought or desire or intention is required to set the process in motion. This might be a prayer, a request to the spirits, or a visualization. Harry Edwards outlined his procedure thus: 'Spend a few moments allowing your mind to picture the patient, dwelling on his personality and the nature of the distress ... simply try to project the picture outwards for the (spirit) guide to receive it.' This is to be followed by a request that those who are listening will be able to correct the condition, so that 'comfort and perfection may return to the sick one'. All limiting thoughts and feelings of doubt should be avoided.[18] Here we see certain obvious similarities with the ideas outlined in this book. For example, Edwards' instructions to picture the patient bears a remarkable resemblance to our concept of visualization. And his advice that all limiting thoughts and doubts are to be avoided unquestionably relates to the fact that such conscious thoughts bring the mind back to the everyday beta level of activity where psychic work is impossible.

One of the most fascinating aspects of a type B/C healing is the subjective experience of the healer and healee. All healings involve feelings akin to love and caring on the part of the healer, but sometimes there is a moment of pure, positive emotion which engulfs both healer and healee. Harry Edwards wrote that the healing experience lifted him 'into a happiness that cannot be described in words'. 'There are,' he said, 'no joys that can transcend the healer's feeling at the moment of knowing that a beneficial result has taken place, and not even years of healing has diminished this.' It is 'quite different to all other human experiences'.[19] I must emphasize that I have had successful healings take place without this intensity of experience. But there is always a feeling of calm and peace, during and after a healing, which seems to be shared by the healee. LeShan described how his healees reported their experiences: 'I felt very calm and peaceful.' 'It was as if I were being tranquilized.' 'It was as if a great wave of warm love came over me.'[20]

If you look back to the last quote of Harry Edwards, you will see that he refers to 'knowing' when the healing has occurred. This relates very closely to the experience of many psychics. Very often, there *is* a moment during psychic work, be it healing, ESP, or whatever, when you know that you have succeeded. At some fundamental level of mind, at that moment, you have psychically achieved your objective. You have no doubt – just a total certainty about the matter. And although this feeling does not invariably occur, it is common enough for you to expect it; just as you should expect to feel at some point, assuming you try psychic healing, the joy of a deep healing experience. People's ability varies, and this may come sooner or later for you. In general, though, the intensity of the healing experience varies. It seems as though it is more intense, the nearer one is to a type C – unfortunately, by all accounts of healing, that appears to be an unpredictable and uncontrollable variable in the complex healing process. Even the acknowledged experts of the healing world have admitted this point. Olga Worrall once said: 'I must emphasize that I have no control over this ability.'[21] Katherine Kuhlman has been quoted as saying that she 'couldn't demand or command God to do anything'. 'In general,' she said, 'I believe it is God's will to heal. But I can't say absolutely what is or is not his will in a particular case.'[22] There are many similar observations.

I suggest that there are certain factors which make a healing more likely: the healer should be relaxed in mind and body, he or she should wish very much that the healing takes place, and he or she should expect that it will do so. Additionally, of course, the extent to which the healer can lower his or her consciousness into the alpha level is important. The instructions on learning to heal at the end of this chapter are designed to make the process as easy as possible, but whether or not you are successful ultimately depends upon a combination of all these factors.

Scientific investigation of a type B healing
To my knowledge, there have been very few experiments on healing at a distance. One such was conducted by Dr Robert Miller of Atlanta, Georgia.[23] He asked the Worralls to conduct a 'distant-prayer' (that is, a healing) on a rye grass seedling while its growth rate was measured by sensitive equipment.

The growth rate of the seedling was stable at about six thousandths of an inch (0.15 mm) per hour throughout 3 and 4 January 1967. The Worralls began their prayer/healing session at 8 p.m. on 4 January. It took the form of visualizing the plant growing as energetically as possible. A careful examination of the chart recording the plant's growth rate, next morning, showed that at 9 p.m. exactly the growth rate had suddenly accelerated. The plant had continued growing faster through the night, to reach a peak growth rate of five hundredths of an inch (1.25 mm) per hour when the trace was examined. Although this experiment was, to say the least, somewhat limited, we do seem to have proof of a potentiating effect which enables organisms to attain the maximum cellular and tissue-level activity of which they are capable.

General discussion
There are several outstanding points which do not conveniently fit into the sections above. They are, however, important to an overall understanding of the healing process. First of all, we can consider the question which was raised at the start of this chapter but has been rather submerged since then: are spirit, psychic and divine healing one and the same thing? Because these different branches of healing overlap in the three-type classification given above, I believe that we *are* entitled to assume they are nothing more than different names for the same processes. The question is, what are those processes? Which explanation is correct?

To suggest that spirits are responsible does not explain how healings actually occur. Indeed, much of what Harry Edwards wrote about spirit healing could equally well be valid whether or not one believed in the existence of spirits. Healing, all in all, fits into a psychic framework consistent with ESP, PK, dowsing and so on, without any need to complicate the matter by discussing 'discarnate beings' on an 'astral plane'. However, having said that, let me quote from *The Psychic Healing Book:*

> In a sense, it doesn't matter which of these theories is more attractive to you. If it seems to you that your psychic abilities are your own, then you will call them up from your deeper consciousness at your own pace and to serve your own needs. If it seems to you that spirits work through you, or that angels guide your steps, then you will call on these other beings for information and assistance. In either case you will work from those levels of your deeper self that we know as the psychic realm.[24]

What, then, of the notion of divine healing? That depends on which concept of God one holds. In the final chapter we shall see that perhaps the explanation for psychic ability and a theory about the nature of God are not incompatible at all.

Earlier I mentioned the factors which might affect the intensity of a healing experience. The next point is closely related to that one: what exactly determines whether a type A, B or C healing takes place? As you may already have gathered, this depends to a large extent on the healer's intentions. The instructions on how to heal at the end of this chapter should make the point clearer.

One question which frequently arises is whether the psychological state of the healee has any effect on the success of a healing. This is a difficult question to answer with certainty. In my opinion, the deeper healings – those nearer type C – occur when the healee is also at the alpha level. But healings do occur even when the healee knows nothing about what is happening. In fact there is probably only one situation in which the healee can actually prevent a healing taking place. Some psychics describe a feeling like 'bouncing off a rubber wall' that occurs when they try to heal someone who does not wish to be healed. This is not indifference or disbelief, but a positive desire not to be healed. It may sometimes be a conscious desire, but much more often it is subconscious. Every doctor knows of the persistent patient who refuses to get better. People do this for various reasons. Maybe they want the love and attention which their illness elicits from other people. Maybe they are frightened of responsibility, and can avoid it by being ill. No doubt there are many, many reasons. But all psychics agree that you can only heal someone else without their conscious agreement or knowledge if, at some deep level of mind, they are willing to co-operate.

Psychic healing techniques form a part of our existence which differs in purpose, basis, and values from everything in our everyday world. You cannot judge psychic and physical techniques by the same standards. And you cannot use them in the same way, either: it is impossible to harm anyone, either deliberately or accidentally, by using visualization techniques.

Learning to heal psychically

The first step in this process is to learn how to relax and go to the alpha level of mind for visualization. Once again, of course, the alternative method of using the five deep breaths as a 'clearing process' is available to you. But the full relaxation and visualization technique will probably produce better results. As ever, the key point is to reduce your conscious thought to the bare minimum necessary for effective visualization. You should not try, in an active sense, to heal; it is more a question of passively allowing your psychic faculty to take charge. If you are in doubt, it may help to re-read Chapter 3.

Before we look at the exercises themselves, a word of warning is in order. In Chapter 7, on psychometry, you may recall that I mentioned the danger of 'taking on' the feelings associated with objects around you. Something similar can happen during psychic healing, only this time you may take on the symptoms of the illness with which you are dealing. (Indeed, some psychic healers do this as a matter of course, later 'curing' themselves of the problem. Such a procedure is quite unnecessary and very undesirable.) Fortunately, there are several ways of preventing this happening. At the alpha level, you can make a conscious decision that you will not accept such symptoms or feelings by thinking: 'I do not wish to take on these symptoms. They are not for me.' Alternatively, you may visualize a white shield of energy all around your body. Simply knowing that this 'psychic shield' is there will prevent you taking on the unpleasant characteristics of your healee's illness. And if you do accidentally pick them up, you can dispel them by visualizing, at the alpha level, a white energy slowly washing your body from top to toes, and then taking all your psychic garbage down into the earth, where it will be neutralized. (See also the introduction to the contact healing method, page 159).

The practice of distant healing

There are four different methods outlined below. You should
soon learn which is more suited to your individual style and
approach. Your first attempts may leave you with the feeling
that you have achieved nothing. But persistence will sooner or
later produce a genuine type B or C healing. Incidentally, it may
be necessary to persevere for some time with a twice daily
visualization. On the other hand, complete recovery may come
quickly. There is, unfortunately, no way of knowing beforehand
what will happen. All the instructions refer to visualization at the
alpha level.

Method A

Choose somebody who is troubled in some way in body or
mind. Visualize them in as much detail as possible in a way that
you are comfortable with. Most people choose to visualize the
person concerned standing against a white or black background.
Now, visualize a beam of powerful white healing energy travelling from your forehead, through space, to surround the healee.
Visualize him or her completely surrounded by this powerful
white energy, with it washing over and soothing and healing
him. Keep this up for ten or fifteen minutes, or until you feel you
have been successful. It may also be helpful, especially with
people who have emotional problems, to visualize the healee
smiling and happy. If possible, ask the person concerned
whether he or she feels any different next time you see them.
This provides a rough and ready check on your success.

Method B

This is a variation of method A. You simply visualize the healee
surrounded with a glowing, vibrant, radiant white healing
energy. This is an 'all-purpose' healing energy which will correct
any mental or physical problem in your healee. At the same
time, you can hold an imaginary conversation with the
individual concerned. You would do this by speaking to him or
her mentally as if you were holding a normal conversation. You
may or may not get the impression that he or she is answering
you back. Your 'conversation' should centre on thoughts of
recovery and other such encouraging matters. You may also
wish to enquire about any problems your healee has, so that you
can deal with them. Some healers feel that they must ask the

healee's permission to conduct a healing. I cannot say that I consider this necessary.

Method C
This involves a different visualization. First you visualize the defective part of the healee's body in whatever way seems most natural. Then you visualize using either your hands or a healing ointment to remove the cause of the problem. You can even imagine some special healing equipment which you feel would be of use in any particular case. (You may not fully understand the idea of helping someone by imagining yourself working inside their body. I should therefore emphasize that this is not supposed to be a way of projecting your soul, spirit or consciousness to another place. It is merely a symbol in the mind which is associated with the mechanism of the healing process itself.) Obviously, you need to have a clear idea of what the trouble is and what visualization you will apply to that problem. There is no limit to the imagery you can use: drilling out deposits in a blocked artery, healing and soothing injuries with an all-purpose ointment, 'seeing' new skin growing across a wound, splicing a bone fracture with healing tape, and so on. Methods like these are described in the books listed in the notes at the end of the chapter.[25]

Some notes on the implications of these exercises
Some people, as you may have read, claim the ability to see an 'aura' or energy field around the human body. When I was discussing psychic healing with a priest in the Church of England, he told me of an occasion when a boy of about fourteen had approached him and asked if it was normal to see a 'light' around people's bodies. The boy said that he could see this for about 80 per cent of the time and, never having heard of the aura, was, not unnaturally, rather upset about it. (It has been claimed that children quite often see the aura until they reach adolescence.) Whether or not this circumstantial evidence is significant is another matter. But it does fit rather neatly alongside traditional descriptions of the aura in psychic literature. Classically, the aura is described as following the shape of the physical body, extending about one foot (30 cm) out from the person's skin. It is supposedly composed of a number of coloured layers which vary with the person's state of health. I offer no judgement on these assertions nor an explanation of

what the aura might be. But one observation is worthy of careful consideration: psychics who claim that they can see the aura report that it decreases in size when a person is ill. And some psychics claim that when two individuals are sending pulses (see page 69), they can see the pulses of energy travel between them and merge into their auras, which increase in size each time an energy pulse is received. This strongly suggests that the aura, if it really does exist, is a 'psychic' energy field around the body. And I would not be surprised if it decreased in size during illness, because this is a time when the natural flow of energy through body and mind is interrupted. Nor would I be surprised to learn that the aura changes in size during psychic healing. We might reasonably suppose that a type A contact healing deplenishes the healer's aura and augments that of the healee, while a type B or C healing replenishes the auras of both healer and healee. The fourth method of distant healing is based upon a psychic examination of the healee's aura.

Method D: Reading the aura

Amy Wallace and Bill Henkin provide instructions for reading the aura and other advanced healing techniques within the framework of an easy-to-follow course of psychic development in *The Psychic Healing Book*.[26] The exercise which I have outlined below owes much to their approach.

As ever, the first step in this procedure is to generate the alpha level of mind. Then you establish a psychic shield around your body and make a conscious decision that this will prevent all adverse influences from reaching you, and prevent your energy from being depleted. Next, decide that you are going to see only the aura. This will avoid confusion. Amy Wallace and Bill Henkin have offered some very sound advice about this technique. They write: 'You needn't strain or exert yourself to see auras. Don't try. Relax, and allow the aura to come to you.'[27] With this advice in mind, here is how you might try the method yourself.

(1) Create a silhouette of your subject as if he was against a white screen.
(2) Let his aura fill the area around his silhouette, at first as a white halo. Observe where it is large and full, where it is thin or if it stops at some parts of the body.
(3) Now allow the aura to become coloured. You may see only

one or two colours at first. Merely watch these colours. Where are they located? Do they move about?

(4) Dissolve the picture and repeat the process. This is to help you develop the ability to see the aura. Note that at first you may think you are just imagining whatever you mentally perceive. However, this is rarely the case. And even if you do create an image and fill in details, they quickly evolve into a truly psychic picture. The key point is that whatever you perceive is probably correct for you. When you are satisfied with your ability to visualize the aura, you can move on to locate illness and pain.

(5) Say to yourself that wherever physical pain exists in the healee's body, a red spot will appear in the aura. Observe the aura until you are satisfied that you have located any red spots.

(6) After locating areas of thickness and heaviness in the aura, and identifying areas of pain, you can start the healing process. First, imagine white healing energy passing around the healee's aura, smoothing out thick areas and augmenting thin ones, until you feel you have a balanced, correct picture.

(7) Then pick the red areas one by one. In the centre of each, imagine a ball of white healing energy gradually growing larger and larger until it has completely filled the red area. Sometimes the areas will not disappear. In this case, leave them be. For some reason the healee probably will not allow those areas to be healed.

Contact healing

I have mentioned that contact healing can produce a draining effect on the healer. To understand this better, we can consider an effect which very often occurs in our everyday lives, but which is nevertheless closely related to the transmission of psychic energy. On occasion, you may meet or visit a person who is depressed, sick or ill. He 'cries on your shoulder' and feels much better an hour later; you, however, feel strangely depressed and exhausted. In cases like these, an undesirable and unintended form of contact healing is taking place. Just as in the process of contact healing itself, one person absorbs the psychic energy of another, and thereby replenishes his or her own depleted resources. This is almost like an automatic process of energy flowing from high to low levels, and has been called the 'psychic vampire' effect. It happens more readily as you develop your psychic ability – unless you take steps to prevent it happening. You can do this by using the psychic shield technique mentioned earlier.

The method of contact healing

Because a type A event alone can produce an unpleasant draining of physical and mental vitality, most experienced and successful healers use a mixed type A/B or A/C. If you wish to heal someone in your presence, this is what you too should aim for. The instructions below are designed to help you achieve it.

First, of course, go to the alpha level in the normal way. Then place your hands on either side of the injured area or position them on the skin over the organ which requires healing. Visualize a white healing energy enveloping both you and the healer. To experience the 'flow of energy' feeling characteristic of contact healing, you may visualize this energy flowing down your right arm, out through your hand, and back up your left hand and arm. Ensure that your hands are not touching each other during this process. The sensations of heat, vibration or cold may not develop for some time, but when they do, they are quite obvious. You can continue for as long as you feel necessary or desirable.

A variation of the technique used for sending pulses (page 69) can be used to calm anyone who is angry, upset or anxious. Instead of touching the person concerned, sit a few feet away with one hand resting on each of your knees. Imagine a white healing energy flowing from your right forefinger, surrounding your subject, and passing back into your left forefinger. It is interesting to try this − after the five deep breaths − without telling the other person what you are doing. To obtain a simple proof that something really does happen when you use this technique, try it on a baby or young child. They spend much of their time at alpha and are especially sensitive to psychic (healing) energy. Another way of demonstrating this is to touch any small cut or bruise on a child's skin for a few moments while imagining a healing energy flow. This often takes pain away and speeds up healing. Of course, you can do the same thing with an adult.

Healing yourself

These techniques can easily be adapted for self-healing. You will need to sit in the usual posture for psychic work and relax in the normal way. Such deep relaxation would, in itself, go a long way to relieve psychosomatic stress problems such as muscular aches, hypertension and stomach ulcers. But you can also use a visualization technique for specific problems, rather like method C above: you visualize recovery and restoration to normal health in a symbolic way. For example, an infection might conjure up an image of invading armies of bacteria and a counter attack by the cells of the body's defence systems. A cut might suggest visualization of cells healing and growing across the wound. Literally, there is no limit to the imagery you can use. One famous researcher in the field encourages people with cancerous tumours to picture the malignant growth as a cauliflower. The body's own defence cells are visualized as piranha fish, which bite chunks out of the cauliflower! It sounds preposterous – but it works. As in the case of hypnagogic imagery (page 80), there is no clear answer as to whether this is a psychic process or not. But there seem to be parallels with the activation of the body's own healing system described by Alexis Carrel as part of a type B healing (page 146).

Additionally, you can use what clearly *is* a psychic technique to heal yourself. This method is a variation of the distant healing technique: you visualize healing energy passing down, over, through your body, flushing out impurity, illness and unwanted material into the earth. This should be done slowly and carefully, in the usual state of mind appropriate to visualization. Simply let the images which you use come to mind and linger there. If they 'float' away, bring them back. Continue doing this for as long as you feel it necessary and beneficial. You should reach a state of mind where you know you have succeeded. A satisfactory alternative is to use the aura reading technique described above in exactly the same way as you did for someone else. This time, however, simply decide that you will see a mental image of your own aura. Then carry out the healing techniques as described in Method D on page 158.

REFERENCES AND NOTES

1   The interested reader will find the clearest account of Harry Edwards' beliefs in H. Edwards, *Spirit Healing* (Herbert Jenkins, London, 1960).

2   This work is described in Thelma Moss, *The Probability of the Impossible* (Routledge and Kegan Paul, London, 1976), pp. 78-83. I have shortened and reworded the points slightly from the original.

3   L. LeShan, *Clairvoyant Reality* (Turnstone Press, Welling-
    borough, 1980), chapter 7.
4   B. Martin, *Healing For You* (Lutterworth Press, London, 1965),
    pp. 154-5
5. H. Edwards, *The Healing Intelligence* (Herbert Jenkins,
    London, 1965), p. 125.
6   LeShan, op. cit., pp. 122-3.
7   Edwards, *Spirit Healing,* op. cit.
8   LeShan, op. cit., p. 124.
9   Reported in LeShan, op. cit., p. 110.
10 Reported in LeShan, op. cit., p. 156.
11 From A. and O. Worrall, *The Gift of Healing* (Harper and Row,
    New York, 1958).
12 H. Edwards, *The Truth About Spiritual Healing* (London
    Spiritualist Press, London, 1956), p. 25.
13 LeShan, op. cit., pp. 112-13.
14 Readers with access to the appropriate journal may like to read
    the original account of the work: *Journal of the American
    Society for Psychical Research,* vol. 61, 1967, 286-305. A more
    accessible account can be found in K. Pedler, *Mind Over Matter*
    (Eyre Methuen, London, 1981), pp. 140-42.
15 Pedler, op. cit., p. 143.
16 Justa M. Smith, *Dimensions of Healing* (Academy of Para-
    psychology and Medicine, 1972), quoted in: Pedler, op. cit., p.
    145.
17 LeShan, op. cit., p. 110.
18 Edwards, *Spirit Healing,* op. cit., p. 45.
19 Edwards, *Spirit Healing,* op. cit., pp. 38-9.
20 LeShan, op. cit., p. 125.
21 Moss, op. cit., p. 81.
22 Moss, op. cit., p. 81.
23 Moss, op. cit., p. 90.
24 Amy Wallace and Bill Henkin, *The Psychic Healing Book* (Turn-
    stone Press, Wellingborough, 1981), pp. 16-17.
25 See, for example, E. H. Shattock, *A Manual of Self-Healing*
    (Turnstone Press, Wellingborough, 1982).
26 Wallace and Henkin, op. cit.
27 Wallace and Henkin, op. cit., p. 101.

13.

Is It Mere Concidence?

Coincidence is defined as 'the accidental concurrence of events which might seem related but are not'. This chapter is designed to show that coincidences are not always accidental; to show that events which *seem* related sometimes occur round about the same time or place because they *are* related — through the human mind's psychic faculty. Many readers will have experienced unexpected series of coincidences. Sometimes such coincidences seem malignant, sometimes benign. Most often they are convenient and beneficial. Here is what Colin Wilson had to say on the subject in his book *The Occult:*

> Certainly there have been enough coincidences in the writing of this book. On one occasion, when I was searching for a piece of information, a book actually fell off the shelf and fell open at the right page. And items of required information have turned up with a promptitude that sometimes made me nervous. After a while I got used to this, and even began to feel a mild resentment when some piece of information evaded me for more than ten minutes or so.[1]

Wilson goes on to suggest that the human mind acts like a 'radar', thus attracting things which are of great concern or interest to one.

At this point, a word of caution is in order. We must be certain, when we actually examine and try to understand what appear to be coincidences, that there is no simple adequate explanation for the events in question. I shall illustrate this point with some examples, because it is important.

In the past, much significance has been given to events that are, in reality, easily explained. For example, you would probably think it extraordinary if you assembled a group of twenty-three people and found that two of them had the same birthday. But in fact probability theory can be used to prove that in any randomly assembled group of twenty-three people, the probability of two having the same birthday is greater than 50 per cent.[2] You would, however, be justified in wondering what was going on if you discovered that there were two people with the same birthday in every group of twenty-three that you assembled. This is because for each group the probability is 50 per cent, or 1 in 2. The probability of this event happening with ten successive groups is less than 1 in 1000.

What do you suppose is the probability of being dealt a complete suit of cards in a card game? The odds against this happening are about 160,000,000,000 to 1. Yet every week 2,000,000 people in England play thirty hands of Bridge. This alone equals more than 3,000,000,000 hands a year. And when all the other card games being played all over the world are added on, you can see that someone, somewhere, is occasionally going to be dealt a complete suit.

Now suppose that you are sitting on a plane travelling across the Atlantic, and you discover that the person sitting next to you lived three blocks away from you when you were children. Such coincidences do happen, and quite frequently, too. Indeed, statisticians play a game called 'The Small World Syndrome', the aim of which is to work out the chances of events like these actually happening. By calculations that would be out of place here, it seems that there is nothing astonishing about these isolated coincidences – they are to be expected rather than anything else. But once again, if a *series* of such events occurred, you would certainly be justified in looking for an explanation that went beyond probability theory. Generally, however, the test of true coincidence is to demonstrate that events which appear to be related are nothing more than statistical certainties. And it is a rigorous test. But it is easy to see that there are many times when 'coincidences' cannot be explained away. As Arthur Koestler put it, intellectual decency demands that we draw a distinction between significant coincidences and trivial ones due to pure chance.[3] Significant coincidences are the ones where we are forced to conclude that the constituent events are related in some way. And from this point, that is the sense in which I shall use the word 'coincidence': to refer to events which are related spatially or temporally or by their very characteristics. In examining some examples of these coincidences, we shall also consider how they might be explained. You will see immediately that these events are of a different order to the sort mentioned above – the sort that can be explained by probability theory.

First of all, then, let us look at the unusual case of George Henry Stanbridge.[4] This man was a newspaper seller who worked at a tube station in North London from 1926 to 1937. He emigrated to Australia in 1958 but returned to London for a holiday in 1977. During his vacation he visited a cinema at which a film called *The Hand of Fate* was showing. Now, here is the unusual part of the story. Remarkably, the plot centred on a newspaper seller called George Henry Stanbridge. This character was depicted as working at the same tube station as the real Stanbridge had used, forty years before. By all accounts, the fictional Stanbridge even looked like the real one! Fortunately the resemblance went no further; in the film the newsman had murdered his wife. (The film distributors withdrew their film when Stanbridge made himself known to them.)

One of the most famous series of coincidences occurred in the months of May and June 1944. Among the solutions to the *Daily Telegraph* crosswords on 3 May, 23 May, 31 May and 2 June respectively were the words: Utah, Omaha, Mulberry, Neptune and Overlord. (The last two were both on 2 June.) The significance of this becomes clear when we consider the following details of the top-secret plan for the Allied invasion of Europe on 6 June: the code word for the overall plan was Overlord; for naval operations, Neptune; for the beaches where the American forces were to land, Utah and Omaha; and for the floating harbours off the Normandy coast, Mulberry. The coincidences were investigated by security officers, who questioned the compiler of the crosswords at great length. Eventually they declared that espionage had been ruled out, and that the matter was a simply a 'coincidence'.[5]

I suspect that many people experience coincidences like the ones mentioned by Colin Wilson. My impression is that such events tend to happen when one is mentally immersed in a particular subject and requires information about it. I shall now describe a typical example of the extraordinary events that may then develop. In 1972 Dame Rebecca West visited the library of the Royal Institute of International Affairs at Chatham House in London to look up details of the Nuremberg war crime trials. She discovered that the trials had been catalogued under arbitrary headings and could not be specifically located. Turning to an assistant, she said: 'I just can't find it. It may be anywhere on these shelves.' For some reason, she then put her hand on a nearby volume, took it out and opened it at random – and there was the very report she wanted! So after hours of fruitless searching, a careless act with no conscious purpose had led to the required report.[6]

I mentioned earlier that coincidences are often convenient and beneficial. In some cases they have even saved an individual from injury or death. At one point in his career, the British actor Sir Alec Guinness found it necessary to work in London on Saturdays. He therefore travelled home to Portsmouth on Sunday mornings by the ten o'clock train. When he went to bed on the Saturday night, he always set two alarm clocks for 7.20 a.m. on the Sunday so that he would have ample time to catch the train. On 3 July 1971 he followed his usual routine and went to bed. However, events did not follow their usual course. First, he had an unusually disturbed night during which he awoke several times. Eventually he dropped off into a fitful sleep from which he awoke at, as he thought, 7.40 a.m. by the alarm clock. He dressed rapidly and set off for his usual mass at eight o'clock in Westminster Cathedral. But when he arrived there was a much larger congregation than usual and Sir Alec began to suspect that something strange had happened. He glanced at his watch and realized that he was attending the nine o'clock service! He had no alternative but to sit through the lengthy sermon. When he returned home and checked the alarm clocks, they turned out to be correct: he had, in fact, misread them when he woke up. Now hopelessly late, he knew that there was no chance of his catching the ten o'clock train. On enquiring at the station about a later train he was told that all trains to Portsmouth were delayed – because of an accident involving the ten o'clock departure.

Apparently the front coach had been derailed and had fallen onto its side. The story is complete when we learn that Sir Alec *habitually* sat in the front coach of the ten o'clock train. Consider what had happened. First, he slept through the alarm clocks. Then, when he did wake up, he misread 8.40 a.m. as 7.40 a.m. and therefore believed that he could attend mass at eight o-clock. But the nine o'clock service – which he actually attended – was of course much longer and made it impossible for him to arrive at the station at ten: a fact which saved him from discomfort or injury, if not death, in the train crash.[7]

How might the four cases above be explained? 'Occam's Razor' is a scientific principle which, loosely interpreted, instructs us that we do not need to postulate complicated explanations if simple ones will suffice. In this case, the simplest explanation is that the events to which I have referred were caused by some form of ESP. The film scriptwriter may have subconsciously and unknowingly derived information from the mind of Stanbridge. The compiler of the *Daily Telegraph* crossword puzzle could have telepathically obtained information from the mind of one or more of the individuals involved in the preparation of the Allied invasion plans. Rebecca West may have been clairvoyant, at least while searching for her reference, and Alec Guinness seems to have precognitively obtained information during his sleep. What makes these cases interesting, though, is that they were all spontaneous and unexpected. Further, the subconscious minds of the individuals concerned had subsequently caused them to act in a way which actually constituted the coincidence: the film scriptwriter incorporated Stanbridge's biography into his film (and, conversely, Stanbridge visited a cinema where that film was showing); the crossword compiler used the code words as solutions to some of his clues; Rebecca West picked the appropriate volume off the library shelves; and Alec Guinness 'just happened' to misread his alarm clocks.

Only two of the cases could be said to have had any obvious purpose, for why should a film scriptwriter and a crossword compiler psychically pick up apparently useless information apparently at random? There is no straightforward answer to this question. One can only speculate that perhaps they were playing some unrecognized but essential part in a larger network of related events.

There is a large group of coincidences where explanations involving ESP do not seem to be adequate. Empirically one sees this in a gambler's 'winning streak' or in the runs of similar events known to those whose work involves contact with many people. Dr Bernard Finch expressed this more precisely in *The Challenge of Chance*: 'If during a surgery or out-patient session, a rare and unusual case turns up, one can guarantee that a similar case will turn up as the second or third patient – or perhaps later during that session.'[8] Shops may quite unexpectedly have a sales run on similar goods – even when this cannot be explained by advertising or promotional offers. Such clustering of events cannot easily be explained. How on earth, for example, would you account for a typewriter shop suddenly receiving many requests for identical repairs to machines of different makes?

One example of this 'clustering' of supposedly random events emerged during the mass telepathy experiment conducted by Sir Alister Hardy at Caxton Hall in 1967 (see page 19).[9] Hardy believed that telepathy could be demonstrated by the transmission from person to person of whole patterns of thought including complex designs and symbols. Two hundred members and friends of the Society for Psychical Research acted as transmitters and twenty as receivers. These twenty were seated in screened cubicles and closely supervised to ensure that they did not communicate with anyone else. While the transmitters concentrated on a picture or slide being displayed to them, the receivers drew or wrote whatever impressions crossed their minds. The pictures and slides were selected at random, so the possibility of fraud was excluded. Altogether, 2112 individual responses were collected for comparison with the target pictures and slides. There were thirty-five direct hits, some of which were very striking indeed. On the face of it, these results are far better than could be accounted for by chance alone, and thus seem to demonstrate that telepathy (or perhaps clairvoyance) was operating.

However, this comparison of response and target pictures was an entirely subjective matter and the investigators needed a control test which would conclusively show that the direct hits really were the result of telepathy and not simply a probabilistic result – that is, one which could be explained by probability theory. (A control acts as a standard of comparison for checking the inferences derived from an experiment.) In this particular case, the control consisted of a series of randomly assembled pictures. Remarkably, within this control group, there was also an astonishingly high rate of correlation. This is astonishing because the random assembling of the control pictures should have produced less, not more, order. The experimenters put it this way: 'We feel that the coincidences in the control groups are of just such a nature as those of the original experiments.' As if this was not enough, the same thing then happened again! During the telepathy experiments, series of diagrams drawn by the receivers bore a strong resemblance, while showing no similarities to the target pictures displayed at the front of the hall. The experimenters assumed that spontaneous telepathy was occurring amongst the receivers, and so arranged another control test. And a clearly demonstrable pattern of similarities emerged yet again. That such order should come out of a randomizing process is a shocking finding: it breaks the laws of physics and probability. Hardy suggested that the runs of coincident drawings in both the telepathy experiments and controls were not the result of chance alone, but were caused by some unknown process of coincidence. This explanation implies that probability theory is at fault – a suggestion which is heresy to modern scientists. Probability theory is widely accepted as having been proved correct. So to suggest that order can emerge from disorder, by some additional process amongst events which have no right, as it were, to 'disobey' clearly mapped probability laws, is a bold step to take.

But such a step had been taken, after a fashion, as long ago as 1919 by the Austrian biologist Paul Kammerer. He spent hours analysing events in his own and other people's lives. His observations confirmed that similar or identical events really do occur in clusters over a short time period or in the same area.[10] (As I suggested before, gamblers call this their winning or losing streak. The phenomenon is also well known to those who deal with the general public.) Thus we now have objective confirmatory evidence of the non-random nature of (at least some) coincidences. How can this be explained? As I explained earlier, one type of coincidence can be attributed to ESP. The problem is to explain the other type of coincidences; the ones like those in Hardy's experiment at Caxton Hall.

Kammerer postulated the existence of a universal force which he called an 'acausal coincidental principle', or ACOP. The ACOP acts upon form and function to bring together objects or events with some affinity for each other. Now, acausal means 'without cause', but conventional scientific doctrine demands that all events must have a cause. Therefore, said Kammerer, we cannot know how the ACOP 'intrudes into the causal order of things' since it is, by definition, outside the laws of physics. Kammerer concluded that, 'we thus arrive at the image of a world mosaic ... which, in spite of constant shufflings and rearrangements, also takes care of bringing like and like together'.

These ideas were later developed by the physicist Wolfgang Pauli and the psychologist Carl Jung. Pauli had already implicitly dealt with acausality when he formulated the 'Exclusion Principle' – one of the many mathematical models needed to maintain the acceptability of quantum theory in physics. The Exclusion Principle determines that no two electrons can occupy the same space. It is a principle for which, as Arthur Koestler put it, 'no justification in terms of physical causation could be invoked . . .'[11] However, one suspects that Pauli's interest in the field of coincidence really stemmed from the fact that all his life he was plagued by mysterious coincidences of one sort or another. It has been reported that he frequently experienced the same sort of event as Rebecca West when he visited libraries (colleagues called this his 'Library Angel'). But his psychic experiences did not stop there. He suffered a malignant poltergeist effect – one of the rare cases experienced by an adult. This normally manifested itself as the spontaneous breaking of equipment when he entered a laboratory. Fellow physicists called this the 'Pauli Effect'. He was not clumsy; quite the contrary. In any case, the apparatus often broke when he was some distance away. On one famous occasion he was sitting in a train at Gottingen railway station when Professor J. Franck in his Gottingen laboratory discovered that a complicated apparatus for the study of atomic phenomena had collapsed! There were many examples of this kind. In terms of the 'repressed hostility' theory of poltergeists, it is interesting to note that Pauli was a theoretical physicist – one wonders whether he subconsciously regarded his more practically biased colleagues with a great deal of hostility.

Jung became interested in the question of coincidence because of some remarkable events during his therapy sessions with his patients. These coincidences seem to have been mainly of the ESP type, a fact which Jung did not notice. But, as a result of his experiences, he and Pauli co-operated on a treatise dealing with coincidence. The extent to which Pauli influenced Jung is not clear. One suspects not much, because Jung's ideas about coincidence are so confused that it is possible to draw only two firm conclusions from his contribution to the treatise:

(1)   His work centres upon the concept of 'synchronicity'. This he defined as, 'the simultaneous occurrence of two or more meaningfully but not causally connected events'. Therefore, by definition, events which occur simultaneously are synchronistic. But Jung decided that precognitive dreams and the event to

which they refer are also synchronistic (even though they are not simultaneous) because 'they are experienced as psychic images *in the present* as though the objective event already existed'.[12]
(2)   Synchronicity stems from the simultaneous occurrence of two mental states: the normal, or causal, one and also one which 'cannot be derived causally from the first'. This action of the mind obviously corresponds to Kammerer's ACOP.

We need not pursue Jung's ideas, because they are totally inadequate and very confusing. To take but one objection, the events which make up a coincidence do not always occur simultaneously. They may occur either together or separately in both time and space. My own explanation for coincidences centres on the proposition that it is the human mind which causes such events. For the time being, we can picture this as a process with many components. At one level, the clairvoyant and precognitive faculties of the mind obtain information which is then passed on to the subconscious, which in turn directs the individual to a certain place and time where events with some particular relevance for him or her will happen. At another level, some telepathic process can alter the attitudes and behaviour of other people in the world, as a result of which favourable circumstances and events are set up. PK may also have a role to play in this, but there is no way of being sure. (Note, however, that we cannot explain the 'clustering effect' this way. Yet ideas of synchronicity and ACOP also seem far from satisfactory.)

Clearly a more detailed picture of the mechanism of coincidence would be useful. However, the implications of the whole process, including the question of causality violation, are best left until the final chapter of this book. As we shall see, explanations for psychic events tend to relate to the whole psychic field, and not just one part of it. At this point our chief concern is with the following question: If coincidences are a result of the activity of the human mind, can they be controlled and brought about as desired?

Let me first recap and clarify my terminology. Coincidences do happen as genuinely random events. One example is the 'coincidence' of finding two people who share the same birthday. This sort of event is presumably a feature of our real, everyday, physical world, and is governed by the laws of probability. At the same time, events which might appear to be nothing more than chance events are, I propose, manifestations of some form of psychic process. Events like these occur in the physical world, but their origins and nature are not easily explained by the laws of the physical world. It is this second type of coincidence with which we are concerned here.

For some reason that is quite unclear, it appears that such coincidences can happen unpredictably in our lives. Rather like spontaneous telepathic contacts, though, we have no way of knowing how, when or why they will do so. Nevertheless, it is possible to gain a greater degree of control over their occurrence, and so use them to our own advantage.

Making coincidences happen

Coincidences which involve ESP can be generated by using the techniques described in other chapters: Chapters 3, 4 and 5 for telepathy clairvoyance and precognition; Chapter 2 for psychokinesis. Other sorts of coincidence are also undoubtedly a reflection of the psychic faculty of the mind and can therefore be achieved by visualization. For example, if you visualize a particular objective, you may begin to experience chains of fortuitous coincidences which seem to lead on to your final objective. As we now know, visualization at the alpha level is a crucial part of any system designed to affect one's relationships and interactions with the physical world. Those who are reading about the power of the mind for the first time may find it hard to accept that one can affect physical events in the world by 'merely' visualizing a particular scene; however, the chapter on psychokinesis should have proved that these techniques are real. You may, even so, want some evidence that this is true. If given that evidence you might say, 'Ah yes, but it won't work for me.' All I can suggest is that you start with some small objective and work up from there. The smaller your initial objective, the less likely you are to doubt that it will actually happen. (Although, conversely, the more likely you are to explain its occurrence as a 'coincidence'. However, if you then recall that the basic proposition of this chapter is that some coincidences are psychic events, you may begin to feel less doubtful.) You could perhaps remind yourself of the emphasis placed on faith by some religions – with faith, 'all things are possible'. Further, as you may know, many mystical and religious systems from widely different cultures have described visualization as a means of affecting the world around us.

You can start with anything. You may have some comparatively small, but important, matter weighing on your mind. Suppose, for example, that you required some information on a particular subject. Your visualization could centre upon seeing yourself obtaining and using that information (but see page 17). Suppose you wished to buy a particular article as a present for someone, but could not find it in any shop. Your visualization might involve seeing yourself finding, buying and giving the object. It is difficult to be specific, because there is literally an infinite variety of situations in which you can use the technique. An obvious question is: How much time needs to be spent visualizing the objective for it actually to happen? This seems to depend upon the 'size' of your objective or the difficulty of attaining it. 'Small' coincidences, or ones which are not particularly difficult to achieve, will probably happen after you use the five deep breaths and visualize briefly – with your eyes open or closed, depending on your ability to work at alpha – the scene which you wish to happen. But 'larger' coincidences, or major objectives, as it is more appropriate to call them, require the full relaxation and visualization exercise for two fifteen-minute periods each day.

I discussed this technique with a friend (who has no interest in psychic events) because I was in doubt about how I should describe it. In fact, I was also testing his reaction to the very idea. But, to my surprise, he immediately knew what I was talking about. 'Ah yes,' he said, 'I know about that. Whenever I am driving into town, I always mentally select the place I wish to park. I then picture myself arriving and parking without any difficulty in that spot. I know that if I allow at least ten minutes before I get there, a space will always be available, and I then dismiss the matter from my mind. Sure enough, there's always a spot free. I've saved a great deal of time and money that way.' Now, the interesting thing is that this person knew nothing of alpha levels and visualization. Yet, because he wanted the technique to work, had total belief in it, and therefore expected that it *would* work, it actually did so. At this point, I am reminded of the story of the woman who prayed to God for a fine day. Then she got off her knees, went to the window and thought: 'Those clouds are a sure sign of rain!' In the same way, trying psychic work will be futile if you neither believe nor expect that it will work.

Manifestation

I approach this subject with some reluctance. To those who know of it, no explanation is necessary. To those who do not, this may not be the best place to start trying to explain it. However, for the sake of completeness, here goes. Manifestation refers to the achievement of major goals through the power of the mind. Once or twice in your life you may have noticed how something you greatly desired turned up quite unexpectedly. This may have appeared to be coincidence, but it is much more likely that your psychic faculty was the cause of the mysterious event. There are people who dismiss this idea, simply saying that it is not a psychic effect at all, that if someone wants something badly enough, he or she will go out of their way to get it. But there is unquestionably more to it than that. Napoleon Hill realized this after he had spent twenty years researching the 'secret' of success that lay behind the achievements of hundreds of the richest men in America. He put forward the results of his research in the book *Think and Grow Rich*.[13] Here is what he wrote near the beginning of that book: '. . . all achievement, all earned riches, have their beginning in an idea.' 'Thoughts are things, and powerful things at that when mixed with definiteness of purpose, persistence and a burning desire for their translation into riches or other material objects.' Hill understood that the subconscious mind had tremendous power, although he did not write in terms of a psychic faculty. Rather, he set out a scheme for the realization of goals and desires which involved something remarkably like the visualization system described in this book. Once again, therefore, we have coincidental confirmation of the tremendous power of the technique when used correctly.

Now let us consider the subject from a wider viewpoint: that of the key steps in attaining any objective. First, you want something to happen. Second, you visualize its appearance. Third, you wait for it to appear. Each of these steps must be undertaken with a particular attitude of mind. You must genuinely want something to happen – not just idly think how pleasant it would be if it did happen. Then, while you visualize your objective, you must believe the process will work – remember that conscious effort or critical consideration takes you from alpha to beta. And lastly, you must expect the process to work, which means having enough faith in it to set a target time or date by which your goal will have been manifested. To borrow an expression from José Silva, the formula for success is *desire, belief and expectancy*. These are simple words, but the ideas behind them can be difficult to grasp. It may therefore be worth looking at what they mean from a different angle.

Desire, we might say, implies not having any doubts about wanting something. Belief, then, implies not having any doubts about the possibility of achieving it. And expectancy implies not having any doubts about it being achieved. In other words, desire, belief and expectancy in alpha constitute an absence of doubt which is so complete that you simply 'know' you can do what you want. That state of mind is achieved during your visualization; but, note well that the 'absence of doubt' is definitely not compatible with conscious thought or effort. It is achieved by visualizing the end result. In all cases, the most important thing is to ensure that you take time and care over the visualization. It should encompass as much detail as you can imagine, and thereby make the scene which you perceive in your mind as vivid and realistic as possible. Suppose you wanted a new car. You would need to picture yourself driving around in it, washing it, and so on. If you need a new job, you would probably want to imagine this series of events: (1) writing a letter of application or seeing an advertisement to which you could respond; (2) attending the interview and everything working out very well; (3) confidently waiting for and opening the letter of acceptance; (4) starting work on the first day. The aim is to generate that moment of 'knowing' which sometimes occurs in psychic work (see page 152). I am not claiming that the process is easy; clearly it is not. And it requires persistence: two periods of fifteen minutes each day at a deep level of mind would probably be adequate. No matter how strange all this seems, you must remember that that is a judgement of the physical, not the psychic world. In the latter, as we shall see in the next chapter, nothing is impossible. For those who would like to read about the power of these psychic techniques, and the results which can be achieved, José Silva's book *The Silva Mind Control Method*,[14] contains many success stories. Another book which illustrates the power of the technique is Napoleon Hill's *Think and Grow Rich*.[15] And Helen Hadsell describes how she developed her psychic abilities specifically with the aim of entering competitions and contests in *The Name It and Claim It Game*.[16]

I should emphasize once again that the key factor in all visualization is not to 'try' or use too much conscious effort. The accuracy of this advice is illustrated by an experience which is fairly common amongst those who set about the development of their psychic ability.

They visualize a certain goal, but fail to achieve it. Then, suddenly, something quite unexpected happens. Casual or random thoughts which crossed their mind while they were not occupied with anything in particular start to become real. That is, events which they can remember casually, rather than purposefully, thinking about in the recent past begin to happen. This demonstrates that the less effort you put in, the more likely you are to achieve results. Now, obviously many random thoughts come into one's mind while one is at alpha. We know and expect this, because alpha is closely associated with daydreaming. The great majority of these thoughts are of no importance − they just float in and out of consciousness. But there may be some thoughts about things which you would very much like to happen. It seems that, under certain circumstances, these can act just as powerfully as a conscious visualization. Unfortunately, those circumstances are difficult to define. Certainly, there must be no criticism, analysis or rejection of the thought. At the same time, there must be some affirmation of the desirability of the event to which it refers. And this must take place at a very subtle level of consciousness, so much so that one only remembers the thought having happened when the event itself does! I cannot offer any more constructive advice on this effect; it is something which one needs to experience and investigate oneself.

The importance of the effect is that it proves the visualization technique is much more effective when conscious thought is minimized. (A word of caution is in order here. You do get what you visualize, so it is essential to ensure that your visualization is desirable and accurate. Equally, it is wise to cancel unwanted thoughts or images which come into your mind at the alpha level. You can do this either by thinking, 'I do not want this to happen', or by mentally drawing a cross through the picture.)

That completes our review of psychic techniques themselves. All that remains now is to try and explain why they work!

REFERENCES AND NOTES

1   C. Wilson, *The Occult* (Granada, London, 1973), pp. 39–40.
2   See any introductory book on statistics.

3   A. Hardy, R. Harvie, A. Koestler, *The Challenge of Chance* (Hutchinson, London, 1973) p. 208.
4   This is reported in J. Taylor, *Science and the Supernatural*, (Maurice Temple-Smith, London, 1975) p. 147.
5   See, for example, Hardy *et al.*, op. cit., pp. 200–201.
6   See Hardy *et al.*, op. cit., p. 162.
7   See Hardy *et al.*, op. cit., p. 172.
8   Reported in Hardy *et al.*, op. cit., p. 194.
9   Hardy *et al.*, op. cit., Part I, pp. 1–118.
10 Kammerer's work was in German, so the easiest way of examining his ideas is to consult A. Koestler, *The Roots of Coincidence* (Hutchinson, London, 1972).
11 See Koestler, op. cit., p. 89.
12 Koestler, op. cit., p. 95.
13 N. Hill, *Think and Grow Rich*.
14 J. Silva and P. Miele, *The Silva Mind Control Method* (Granada, London, 1980).
15 Hill, op. cit.
16 Helen Hadshell, *The Name It and Claim It Game*.

14.

Towards An Understanding
of the Psychic World

In Chapter 10, I demonstrated that well-established laws of physics about the properties of matter and energy have not provided a framework within which scientists have been able to explain ESP and dowsing. As we consider other psychic events, in the order in which they are set out in this book, it becomes even harder to devise reasonable explanations. Telepathy could perhaps have been explained by postulating some kind of 'radiation', of a sort not yet defined, which permitted mind-to-mind communication. But precognition, clairvoyance, PK and dowsing cannot be explained so glibly. And what of the problems for our concept of time flowing from past to present to future? As if this was not bad enough, there is the added difficulty of explaining the amazing and dramatic events involved in psychic healing and visualization. But in fact the situation is not so hopeless as it might at first appear. ESP cannot, it is true, be explained in terms of classical physics, but there have been many attempts by atomic and nuclear physicists to show that ESP is theoretically possible.

This branch of physics is chiefly concerned with the relationship between matter and energy at the atomic level: a level at which day-to-day reality becomes much less clearly defined. To take but one example of this, the electron has been shown to have the properties of both an energy wave and a small particle. It is, in part, because scientists have grappled with such extraordinary ideas that they are willing to consider psychic phenomena which break the laws of classical physics. In the words of Arthur Koestler: '... the unthinkable phenomena of ESP appear somewhat less preposterous in the light of the unthinkable propositions of physics.'[1] Oddly enough, though, most of the theories formulated by nuclear or atomic physicists do not really solve the problem of explaining ESP. For one thing, they are based upon the complex mathematical formulations of quantum theory, and thus beyond the grasp of most people. Moreover, they tend to be incapable of proof or rebuttal: they are purely theoretical. This is not to say that they are incorrect, of course, rather that their practical usefulness is limited. And it is for these reasons that I have not attempted to review all of them. Nevertheless, for a hint of the kind of work which I am talking about, we may examine the ideas of Adrian Dobbs, a Cambridge physicist who died in the early 1970s.

Dobbs produced a hypothesis which proposed the existence of a five-dimensional universe; it comprised three spatial dimensions, to which we are accustomed, and two dimensions of time to which we are not. The theory is so complicated that I can only follow Arthur Koestler's lead here. As he explains it, 'the anticipation of future events [precognition] follows the second time dimension, where "objective probabilities" play the same part as causal relations in classical physics'. In other words, the probability of various events occurring in the future are contained as 'dispositional factors' in a second time dimension. These factors 'incline the future to occur in certain specific ways'.[2] Clearly, to have an idea of what the future holds, as we seem to in precognition, we must have knowledge of these dispositional factors. But they cannot be observed or deduced because they occur in a second time dimension. In fact, information about them is conveyed to us by a hypothetical particle called a 'psitron'. Psitrons have some rather strange properties. But there are precedents for strange particles in physics. For example, the neutrino has been accepted as a valid and meaningful concept for many years by physicists, and evidence for their existence has been obtained. Yet the neutrino has no mass, no charge, no magnetic field and passes straight through the earth. In Dobbs' hypothetical scheme, psitrons can affect the brain directly. They might do this by triggering brain nerve cells poised just below their level of activation. When one nerve cell is triggered in this way, it could perhaps set off a chain reaction in other nerve cells and so affect large areas of the brain.

Dobbs' theory related to telepathy, clairvoyance and precognition, for the properties of the psitron allow instant and unlimited communication through the psychic faculty. Note, however, that no one can claim this theory is correct; there are many others which are equally plausible. The point is that nuclear (or more accurately, 'quantum') physicists have found parallels between their work and the implications of ESP; and because they have found such parallels, they have tried to explain ESP. What is the importance of this, though, if their theories cannot be proved right or wrong? Arthur Koestler has written:

> I talked earlier on of a *negative* rapprochement between quantum physics and ESP, in so far as the surrealistic concepts of the former make it easier to suspend disbelief in the latter; if the former is permitted to violate the 'laws of nature' as they were understood by classical physics a century ago, the latter may claim the same right. But to stress the point once more, this is merely a negative agreement, a shared disregard for ancient taboos, for a mechanistic world-view which has become an anachronism.[3]

We must now move beyond this approach to ESP and consider other psychic effects; in particular, PK and healing. Even amongst those who accept the idea of ESP, PK and healing are regarded with much more caution. This is because you cannot influence the physical world of macroscopic objects with theoretical particles which have no mass, electric charge or other such properties. But what does this mean in practical terms? Arthur Koestler has said that although we must accept the evidence for such phenomena, we must also give up hope of any physical explanation – 'even in the terms of the most advanced and permissive quantum mechanics'. But there is, I think, more to the problem than that. We know from personal experience that ESP, dowsing, precognition, healing and PK are all different aspects of the same psychic faculty within each one of us. Any explanation of ESP should therefore be adaptable to explain PK and healing (and vice versa). As a result of this requirement it is highly improbable that we can actually formulate a theory which tells us exactly how such effects occur. Rather, we are looking to establish a framework within which all psychic events are feasible. *That* is what is meant by 'Towards An Understanding'. Our first step in doing this is to examine certain ideas in physics and consider their implications. I have kept the material as simple as possible, and it should not be difficult to follow.

First of all, consider the concepts of time and space. In our everyday, rational world, we believe that time flows sequentially. We believe we can measure space and that we know what it is –

the place where objects are not, as it were. Moreover, time and space seem to be absolute – that is, each one seems to exist without any necessary relationship to the other. However, this is an illusion. Time and space vary according to where you are and what you are doing.

The simplest illustration of this idea is related to the fact that electromagnetic radiation travelling across space takes a finite time to reach Earth. Let us assume that it is possible for the human eye to resolve this light and thus actually see any events taking place on, say, Mars. In fact, because it takes ten minutes for light from Mars to reach Earth, we can never see what is happening on that planet at the moment we look at it. Equally a 'Martian' watching events on his own planet can never watch them at the same time as a man on Earth: it is impossible, because light from those events reaches him long before it reaches Earth. But who has the real 'now'? Each man thinks that what he sees on Mars is happening 'now' – as he looks at it. This time-delay occurs even at very small distances, though the limitations of our senses mean we cannot perceive it.

The conclusion derived from reasoning like this was Einstein's concept of 'space-time'. What does this mean? Simply that talking about space and time as two separate entities is meaningless. The advanced physics required to define space-time clearly has no place in a book like this. Instead, let us consider a situation in which we can intuitively understand the usefulness of the concept. This situation is called the 'twin paradox'.

A twenty-five-year-old man on Earth listens to radio signals sent at ten-minute intervals by his twin brother, who is in a stationary spacecraft in space. One sends and the other receives a signal every ten minutes, but even now the time of sending and receiving are separated because of the distance the radiation has to travel. Suppose now that the spacecraft accelerates away from Earth and begins to move at a speed approaching the speed of light. The man on board still sends signals every ten minutes by his 'space' scale of time. He lives his life at a normal rate. But his twin on Earth feels his astronaut brother has not been careful enough. The earthbound twin is noticing a longer and longer time between receiving signals. He does not know that this is because each signal the spacecraft sends has much further to travel and so takes longer (remember, the craft is accelerating away from the earth). For example, the space-twin sends three signals in thirty minutes. But the earth twin receives them in one hour: *which means he must be ageing faster than his brother.* Twenty space-years later, the spacecraft returns to earth: the men are still twins but one is forty and the other sixty!

The significance of this is shocking: time is flexible – it depends on where you are and on what you are doing. This is not a method of explaining precognition, but it does help to show that the qualities of temporal flexibility required for precognition are not unthinkable, even in our 'real' world. So here we have two concepts of space and time, two frames of reference by which to analyse and understand the world around us. The first dictates our existence in the everyday world of physical objects and temporal sequences; the second does not have separate concepts of time and space, we cannot see it or understand it, nor does it seem to affect our lives – yet it co-exists with the other one.

Consider now the structure of matter. The original model of the atom formulated at the beginning of this century proposed that the atom had a central nucleus of protons and neutrons, around which electrons circled in an orbit, like planets in the solar system around the sun. But this model quickly ran into difficulties. Atomic physicists realized that the observable properties of the electron did not correspond with this model. The idea was abandoned, and replaced with a mathematical theory. In the words of Arthur Koestler, this theory 'got rid of the worst paradoxes – but at the price of renouncing any claims of intelligibility or representability in terms of three-dimensional space, time, matter or causation'.[4] The theory produced the 'Principle of Complementarity': simplistically, this means that electrons may behave as either solid particles or wave-like energy, depending on the circumstances. Werner Heisenberg observed that:

> ... the concept of complementarity is meant to describe a situation in which we can look at one and the same event through two different frames of reference. These two frames mutually exclude each other, but they also complement each other, and only the juxtaposition of these contradictory frames provides an exhaustive view of the appearances of the phenomena.[5]

In other words: matter, although obviously solid in our real, everyday world, can equally well be thought of as an insubstantial energy form.

As another example of the problems of modern physics, we can briefly examine the 'Uncertainty Principle'. Looking around in the world about us, we feel that we see things as they are. But it is possible to argue along quite different lines. To understand this, we need to go back to the origins of the Uncertainty Principle and consider its formulation and implications.

Heisenberg's Principle of Uncertainty is a precise mathematical argument, formulated to analyse the behaviour of sub-atomic particles. Heisenberg discovered that it is impossible to measure both the position and the momentum of an electron. Although you can know one quantity accurately, that measurement blurs the other. This principle could be interpreted in another way: to observe is to disturb. It seems preposterous to suggest that by looking at an object in the universe, we alter or disturb that object (and thereby alter the universe itself). The most obvious answer to this objection is that macroscopic objects in the everyday world are not affected by disturbances produced by observation. But as F.A. Wolf points out, if we choose to regard our existence within the framework of quantum physics, then every time we look at an object, we are to some extent making a construction of reality: the universe changes each time we alter our method of observation! 'At the quantum level ... reality becomes both paradoxical and sensible at the same time. Our acts of observation are what we experience as the everyday world.'[6] Clearly, here are two frames of reference by which we can regard the world: first, that everything is fixed, determinate, unchanging; or, that reality is made manifest in a way that depends upon the very act of 'looking at' or 'being in' the world.

As yet another example of the problems which physics has in defining the properties of the world around us, there is the 'Principle of Local Causes'. This states, in essence, that events occurring in one place in the universe cannot affect events in any other place unless there is some material or energy link between them. It is a principle which intuitively seems correct. However, calculations which suggest that the principle can fail have been put forward. In 1964, the physicist Dr John Bell wrote an entirely theoretical paper, in which he came to the astonishing conclusion that if quantum theory is correct, then the Principle of Local Causes is not universally true. Bell's theorem proposes that particles which were once in contact continue to influence each other, no matter how far apart they move. This influence acts instantaneously – even if the particles are at opposite ends of the universe. Now, the problem is that such an 'influence' would have to be transmitted faster than the speed of light (instantaneous influence is infinitely quick, whereas the speed of light is finite – 186,000 miles per second). But quantum physics relies upon the assumption that no energy can move faster than the speed of light. So what is this 'influence'? I shall try to answer that question in a moment. What is important here is that by working from the accepted viewpoint of a reality where causality reigns supreme (as the Principle of Local Causes), we come to a reality where causality fails and separate events can influence each other.

A final example of the diverse views of the world which have been presented in recent years is Dr David Bohm's view of an 'implicate' universe. The implicate is the most fundamental level of existence, composed of a spaceless, timeless realm in which space, time, matter and energy are unified into a single universal level of existence. This implicate realm contrasts sharply with our everyday, or 'explicate', world. Objects in the explicate world are constantly materializing out of the implicate, he suggests. How, then, is it that we see our world as a stable, consistent reality? One analogy is the movement of cine film through a projector.[7] For about half the time a film is running, the black spaces between the film frames are in the light path of the projector. Despite this, we still see the film as a continuous moving image. In the same way, our everyday perception of the world is one of stability and continuity. Thus, yet again, we have a theoretical proposition of two realities, where we might imagine only one exists.

Now, there are some obvious points to be made about these different ideas. Either separately, or in combination, they could form a plausible explanation of one or more psychic phenomena. Note that the ideas were not formulated for that purpose; they were all put forward to explain gaps and anomalies in existing knowledge.

First of all, let us take the subject of 'coincidences'. Bell's theorem, if you recall, proposes that particles once in contact continue to influence each other, no matter how far apart they are. The influence between them cannot, by the laws of quantum physics, be energy; is it possible to reconcile quantum physics with the Bell theorem? It is if you propose that the influence is consciousness itself. But how consciousness might act in this role is another matter. (To be fair, I should mention it is not actually certain that Bell's theorem applies to acausal events in the macroscopic, rather than the quantum, level of reality.)

An obvious point in this discussion is that psychic events require us to abandon the belief that time flows from past to future. Or, more accurately, psychic events must be explained in a framework which contains no reference to time as we know it. Even so, the relationship of psychic work to the everyday world must involve time, since time as a reality is an integral part of that world. David Bohm's timeless implicate fulfils this requirement. In this theory, the instant communication which we believe is involved in telepathy, the act of precognition and the rapid physical changes involved in some healings are no longer 'impossible' events.

Healing itself we may consider to be a form of psychokinesis: the power of 'mind over matter' extends from dice-throwing to metal-bending, poltergeists, rapid changes in the structure of the body, and no doubt many other areas as well. David Bohm's idea of an implicate universe is highly relevant here. He proposes that all matter is being materialized from a unified field 'beyond', yet co-existent with, our physical world. Further, energy itself is a part of that unified field, and so one might propose that matter takes a form which depends upon the energy or information available. Now, thoughts are a form of energy or information. Conceivably, therefore, a thought could influence the form of matter; hence – metal-bending and other PK effects.

David Bohm's work also suggests that we may regard acausal coincidences as 'ordinary' events. The rationale is this: in the implicate world, all is one, all events are connected. So information exchange is not merely possible, it is unavoidable. The information generated in one mind could therefore be available to other minds; equally, it could influence the form in which objects become material and the way in which events occur – even at widely separated places in the universe. Thus, what appear to be acausal events in the material world are in fact 'linked' in the implicate.

Another way of looking at these problems can be deduced from Heisenberg's work on the Uncertainty Principle. The propositions derived from Heisenberg's work are that 'to observe is to disturb' and that 'to observe is [in a sense] to construct reality'. Yet *all* realities are potentially present in nature; even what is obscured by the very act of observation is still potentially present (notice the similarity with Bohm's work). Heisenberg called this potential reality an 'intermediate reality'. The point is that all potential reality is available to us. What we experience as reality depends on what we choose to see, and think, and do. Fred Wolf puts it this way:

> Every act we perform is a choice, even if we are unaware that we have made a choice. Our unawareness of choice at the level of electrons and atoms gives us the illusion of a mechanical reality. In this way ... we appear to be victims ... ruled by a destiny we did not determine.[8]

The possibility of controlling those choices so as to make reality occur in a particular way might be the basis of being able to establish coincidences by the visualization process.

It is now time to step back metaphorically and consider the contrasting viewpoints of reality which have been described in this chapter, and also what they *mean*.

Ways of looking at the world

Here are the contrasting views of reality which I have set out so far in this chapter.

From the viewpoint of everyday reality	*From an alternative viewpoint of reality*
Space and time are separate, well-defined and absolute.	Space and time are inextricably linked and not absolute.
Electrons and atomic particles are solid.	Electrons and atoms may behave as particles or energy waves.
Reality is fixed.	Reality depends on the act of observation.
Causality is an established law of nature. Events in one part of the universe cannot affect unconnected events elsewhere.	Particles once in contact continue to influence each other, no matter how far apart they may be.
One object or event can only affect another if they are linked physically or by the transmission of energy.	Consciousness itself may act as a means of influence between two events.

It seems fairly clear that these points all add up to two different but coherent views of the world – or reality. The first view defines the physical world which we perceive with our everyday senses – the 'sensory' world. The second viewpoint was put forward by scientists to explain anomalies and inconsistencies in nuclear physics. Yet it also seems to offer a framework in which psychic events might take place without breaking established laws of nature in the sensory world. Interestingly, the conclusions arrived at by different scientists (Einstein, Heisenberg, Bohr, Bell and Bohm) are all complementary: they point in the same direction. They describe similar characteristics of this second reality. Because this reality is one in which psychic events could occur, I shall call it the 'Psychic Reality'. To develop this discussion, it is now necessary to leave the physicists for a short while, and turn to the work of Lawrence LeShan, whom I first introduced in the chapter on healing.

A scientific study of psychics and mystics

LeShan has applied the scientific method to his study of the psychic world. He realized that previous studies had concentrated on the question: 'How is information transmitted during ESP?' and failed to find an answer. So instead, he asked, 'What is going on when psychic events occur? What is the structure of the total situation when psychic events occur?'[9] He studied this by the simple method of asking people with psychic ability to describe their feelings when they received information psychically. All of them mentioned a 'shift of awareness' at the moment of psychic work. And they were able to define clearly the characteristics of that state of awareness.[10] During psychic work, they said:

(1)   The relationships between entities are more important than the differences between them. Or, to put it another way, 'everything – including you and me – is primarily and fundamentally related to and a part of everything else'.
(2)   Time does not exist as we understand it in the sensory world – all events, past, present and future, simply 'are'. .
(3)   Events are beyond (this is a metaphor) the judgements or descriptions which we apply in the sensory world. Good, bad and evil are concepts which are irrelevant to perceptions made during psychic work.
(4)   There is a better way of gaining information than through

the senses. This is because everything is fundamentally related to everything else. At the moment of knowing and accepting this oneness as a fact, there is nothing to bar the exchange of information between two individuals.

After this exercise, LeShan examined mystical systems and traditions.[11] Mysticism is the belief in the attainment through meditation, contemplation, or the like, of 'truths' inaccessible to normal understanding. It is clearly a spiritual pathway; that is, the truths sought after concern the nature of God or some similar concept of an Absolute. All mystics aim to achieve a state of mind in which these truths become clear to them. The characteristics of moments when a mystic feels that he has achieved that desirable state of mind were analysed by Bertrand Russell.[12] He found agreement between all mystical traditions on these points:

(1)   That there is a better way of gaining information than through the senses.
(2)   That there is a fundamental unity to all things.
(3)   That time is an illusion.
(4)   That all evil is mere appearance.

LeShan points out how closely these characteristics resemble his analysis of the psychic's experience at the moment when psychic work is effected. What, we may well ask, are the implications of this similarity?

As far as we are concerned, they are that man is 'capable of perceiving the world as put together in two different ways'.[13] LeShan quotes Evelyn Underhill, a Christian mystic, who expressed the point precisely:

> Now it is a paradox of human life, often observed by the most concrete and unimaginative philosophers, that man seems to be poised between two contradictory orders of reality . . . two ways of apprehending existence lie within the possible span of his consciousness. That great pair of opposites which metaphysicians call Being and Becoming . . . and others mean, when they speak of the Spiritual and the Natural Worlds . . .[14]

LeShan has termed the framework within which psychics and mystics view the world at moments of psychic awareness or during mystical experiences the *Clairvoyant Reality*. This reality contrasts with the Sensory Reality, that is, the one in which we live during our everyday lives. LeShan's Clairvoyant Reality obviously corresponds to what I earlier called the 'Psychic Reality' when I described the research of twentieth-century physicists.

The threads come together

And now you may have grasped the link between the material which formed the first section of this chapter and the work of LeShan. All in all, we have the evidence of three different groups of people for the fact that the Clairvoyant and Sensory Realities co-exist: psychics, who speak from an experiential position; mystics, who speak from traditions which go back many centuries; and physicists – a hard-headed, rational bunch of men. Although I have not mentioned the fact, LeShan's attempts to explain psychic events included not only a review of the work of psychics (or mediums, as he prefers to call them) and mystics, but also a review of the writings of twentieth-century physicists. It is interesting to note that LeShan's analysis of the work of these physicists is rather different to mine, but we have both arrived at the same conclusions. Whereas I have tried to illustrate the reasons why it became necessary for physicists to propose a 'different' reality, LeShan quoted from what scientists had written when they were discussing their research and theory. In doing so, he quoted passages which directly relate to the four characteristics of the Clairvoyant Reality which featured in the psychics' and mystics' world view. It is not my intention to cover material which has been so lucidly presented before, so I shall restrict myself to one example for each of the four points. Remember that these are physicists' words:

(1)   That all things have a fundamental unity:

> According to modern mechanics [field theory], each individual particle of the system, in a certain sense, at any one time, exists simultaneously in every part of the space occupied by the system.[15] (Max Planck)

(2)   That the flow of time is an illusion:

> In man's brief tenancy on earth he egocentrically orders events in his mind according to his own feelings of past, present and future. But except on the reels of one's own consciousness, the universe, the objective world of reality, does not 'happen' – it simply exists.[16] (Lincoln Barnett)

(3) That descriptive judgements are irrelevant in the Clairvoyant Reality:

> To know physical reality is to know where to look when something is wanted or needed to be seen; it is to be able to cure when a cure is desired, to kill when killing is intended. But natural science will never tell whether it is good or bad to look, to cure or to kill. It simply lacks the premise of an 'ought'.[17] (Henry Margenau)

(4) That there is a better way of gaining information than through the senses:

> Since, however, sense perception only gives information of this external world or of 'physical reality' indirectly, we can only grasp the latter by speculative means.[18] (Einstein)

We are all accustomed to thinking in terms which do not take account of the existence of two realities: as far as most of us are concerned, what exists in the Sensory Reality is the extent of reality. And when we are presented with evidence which suggests that two complementary realities exist, we may react with scepticism: 'If the Clairvoyant Reality exists, show it to me! Where is it?', or alternatively, 'If two realities exist, and there are two ways of looking at the world around us, which is correct? Which is better?' I shall attempt to deal with these points in the order in which they are presented.

To ask where the Clairvoyant Reality is located is to misunderstand the nature of the reality thus named. By definition, it is 'beyond' our ordinary sense organs, which can perceive only the Sensory Reality. But if we cannot see, touch, taste, smell or hear the Clairvoyant Reality, how do we get in contact with it? By using and developing our psychic sense. That is the purpose of this book. (Mystical systems place a different emphasis on the development of the psychic sense. They are not oriented towards 'paranormal' or psychic techniques, but towards a loftier spiritual peak. In either case, though, the basic philosophy is the same.) Indeed, the psychic sense is the doorway to the Clairvoyant Reality. That reality does not have a location because it is 'beyond' space and time; it is a state of being. For those who are still floundering with this concept, I can add an analogy. We know that the constituent particles of the atom can behave either as energy waves or particles. However, this duality is impossible to determine with our ordinary sense organs; all we see is the 'hard-edged face' of particles making up solid objects. Yet the chair on which you sit or the desk on which I write is, in another sense, an insubstantial energy form. Both views are valid; they co-exist; they are complementary; and one cannot exist without the other.

Which view of reality is better depends on what you want to do. In the words of Lawrence LeShan:

> Both are equally valid even though they are quite different. Which one is chosen at a particular time does not depend on which is more true, but on what you are trying to accomplish at that particular moment . . . [the Sensory Reality] is the reality in which one can select goals, and plan and carry out action. It is a reality we *must* learn to operate in in order to stay alive physically . . . If, however, instead of the necessary, practical goals of the biological and physical world which we can work toward so well in the Sensory Reality, we wish to work toward another type of goal, we need the Clairvoyant Reality. If we wish to choose as our goals a sense of serenity, peace, joy in living, being fully at home in the cosmos, a deeper understanding of truth, our fullest ability to love, we need the world of the One. Beyond this, however, is the crucial fact that to attain our full humanness we need both.[19]

To which we add, the Clairvoyant Reality is necessary for psychic work.

Understanding psychic work in the framework of the Clairvoyant Reality

The basic assumption behind all of the rest of this chapter is that during psychic work we gain access to the Clairvoyant Reality. This is done by lowering consciousness to the alpha level of mind. In this book, we have seen how relaxation and visualization can alter levels of consciousness. Other methods include prayer, contemplation and meditation. But *why* does the alpha level provide us with access to the Clairvoyant Reality? The answer seems to be that there are remarkable parallels between the characteristic features of the alpha level of mind and the properties of the Clairvoyant Reality:

(1) At the alpha level, one's feeling of self is reduced. Awareness of one's own body and mind are reduced as attention is directed on to the particular matter with which you are concerned. (This relates to the suggestion that in the Clairvoyant Reality, the links between objects and events are more important than the differences between them. It also has a hint of the idea 'all is one'.)

(2)   Judgements cannot be made at the alpha level, for critical analysis or reasoning take one back to the normal sensory world of beta activity. Hence, words like 'good' or 'evil' have no relevance. (This relates to the suggestion that value judgements are irrelevant to the Clairvoyant Reality.)

(3)   The normal senses are less active and important at the alpha level because they cannot help with psychic work. For example, telepathic communication takes place at a subtle level of consciousness and involves what I have called the psychic sense. (This relates closely to the suggestion that in the Clairvoyant Reality, there is a better way of gaining information than through the senses.)

(4)   At the alpha level, one tends to lose awareness of time. If you have learnt to function deeply at alpha with your eyes open, you may be able to look at a clock or watch face and find that the second hand seems to have stopped moving. Of course, the hand has not stopped moving in the objective, sensory, beta world; the point is that your subjective sensation of time at different levels of consciousness is quite different. As you go deeper into alpha, time seems to slow down progressively. This effect can only be managed by those with a fair degree of control over their consciousness. However, Itzhak Bentov set out a simple experiment in his book *Stalking the Wild Pendulum*,[20] which allows nearly everyone to experience the effect which the alpha level has on time. The only equipment needed is a clock or watch with an easily visible second hand. I have simplified the instructions somewhat.

Step 1   Relax and position the watch so that you can see it with no difficulty through half-closed eyes.

Step 2   Look at the watch in a relaxed way. Follow the second hand; absorb its rhythm. This must be done effortlessly.

Step 3   Close your eyes. Visualize yourself engaged in your favourite activity. This visualization has to be so total that you actually feel yourself to be a part of the scene you imagine. Choose a relaxing activity, not a hectic one.

Step 4   When you have stabilized this visualization, slowly open your eyes slightly. *Do not focus on the watch*, just let your gaze fall on the dial as though you are a disinterested observer. 'If you have followed the instructions properly, you may see the second hand

> stick in a few places, slow down, and hover for quite
> a while.'[21]

This does not mean that the movement of the clock has been slowed; it just means that one's subjective time has been altered. Clearly, however, this strange effect must be linked with the suggestion that in the Clairvoyant Reality, the flow of time is an illusion.

Critical readers may ask whether a comparison between the observable properties of the alpha level and the properties of the Clairvoyant Reality is really *proof* that one is in fact associated with the other. I believe the link is clear: the framework derived from theoretical physics links to experiential reports of psychics and mystics, and to the observable properties of the mind at the alpha level *so well* that there can be little doubt of a very close association of the form outlined here. (Although ultimately, of course, we do not know *how* the mind at the alpha level becomes one with the Clairvoyant Reality.)

Let us complete our study of the psychic world by examining more closely the way in which particular psychic techniques might be explained in the framework of the two realities.

Understanding ESP, dowsing and divination

In the Clairvoyant Reality, all is one. Space cannot, therefore, be a hindrance to the exchange of information between people or between people and objects. Time does not exist, so this cannot be a barrier, either. Thus we have a theoretical basis for the existence of telepathy, clairvoyance, precognition, psychometry, dowsing and divination. Bearing in mind that I am currently referring to those categories of psychic experience, it is easy to extend the discussion.

The idea of the Clairvoyant Reality is difficult to accept, naturally. We live in the sensory world, and find it difficult to believe in ESP, let alone a second reality! But the concept of the Clairvoyant Reality *feels* so right that we must consider it carefully. The first point which arises concerns the limitations of our psychic faculties. If 'all is one' in the Clairvoyant Reality, then theoretically an unlimited amount of information is available to our psychic sense. Yet we have to work on our psychic faculties to improve them, so clearly something normally prevents our gaining access to this information. The explanation lies, partly, in the interaction of our conscious and subconscious minds. As I have mentioned in a previous chapter, the subconscious does not present all the information available to our sense organs to consciousness. If it did, we would be overwhelmed. Presumably the same is true of information provided by our psychic sense. But, more importantly, we do not actually attain a 'pure' state of Clairvoyant Reality when working psychically. Thus far, I have implied that all psychic work occurs in a more or less pure state of Clairvoyant Reality in which all self-awareness is suspended. But this, of course, could not actually be the case, because all psychics need to be aware of their thoughts and mental activity during psychic work. The reason for this is obvious: it is our conscious orientation towards a certain objective, both before and during psychic work, which enables us to direct our minds to the achievement of that objective. We must always have consciousness at some level, even though that level is an 'altered state'. Also, of course, one could not report or remember what had happened during psychic work if consciousness was completely suspended. In passing, we may note that the pure state of Clairvoyant Reality probably corresponds to the mystics' nirvana or heaven or cosmic consciousness. It is a state which mystics find hard to describe in the language of the Sensory Reality, but one common feature of all their descriptions is the fact that 'all knowledge is available to an individual'. This corresponds exactly with the properties of the Clairvoyant Reality. Although most of us cannot even imagine what the pure Clairvoyant Reality is like, we can obtain glimpses of it when we use our psychic faculty.

Understanding coincidences

As we have already seen, coincidences which are induced by the psychic powers of the human mind appear to be acausal events in the Sensory Reality. ESP and PK have some role to play in these coincidences, as I described in Chapter 12, but that is probably not the whole story. I mentioned on page 186 that coincidences may result from our ability to control the form of events by the very way in which we think. This idea can be developed further. If one equates Heisenberg's concept of an 'intermediate' or 'potential' reality with LeShan's concept of a Clairvoyant Reality, one 'produces' a non-sensory reality in which, at any moment, the future is made up of an infinite number of possible events, each of which has a different probability of occurring. When an individual then visualizes his chosen event, or 'probability', he can make that event into a reality – even though it is in the (sensory world's) future. This is because, at the moment of psychic work, that choice becomes the reality which is, will be, and always has been. (In practice, whether or not one succeeds in this depends on the extent to which one has been able to gain 'access' to the Clairvoyant Reality.) It is therefore not at all paradoxical to state, as LeShan has done, that there cannot be free will or choice in the Clairvoyant Reality.

Understanding type B psychic healing

LeShan has considered whether the framework of Clairvoyant Reality can account for type B psychic healing. In doing so, he analysed reports by successful healers of how they felt during the healing experience. All the reports pointed to a moment of altered consciousness during which the psychic healing actually occurred. LeShan has written:

> It seemed only to take a moment, a moment of such intense knowledge of the Clairvoyant Reality structure of the cosmos that it filled consciousness entirely, so that there was – for that moment – nothing else in the field of knowing to prevent the healing results from occurring.[22]

(Here we have a beautiful confirmation of the 'moment of knowing' you have been successful in psychic work, of which I have written before.) It seems that the most successful healers are regularly able to operate in the Clairvoyant Reality to this degree. Although perhaps few of us will be able to enter the Clairvoyant Reality to such an extent regularly, the method by which we all heal is based on the same principle: that is, we operate – for a time – at a level of mind somewhere between the Sensory and Clairvoyant Realities. When we do so, the body healing systems of the healee seem to work at a level nearer their true potential. But *why* do they do so? LeShan suggests that the explanation relates to a Christian Science analogy used to 'explain' this type of healing:

> Christian Scientists point out that a rubber ball retains its usual shape of roundness (here the analogy for 'health') so long as there is no pressure to deform it (here the analogy for 'illness'). As soon as the pressure is released, it springs back to roundness. The pressure, they say, is being cut off from God, is the lack of the knowledge that one is a part of God, or, in our terms, the All. When this 'pressure' is 'released' through the healer setting up a metaphysical

system where the healee is included in the All . . . the healee's body responds by a tendency to repair itself and work towards health.[23]

The relationship of psychokinesis and other types of healing to the Clairvoyant Reality concept

I have suggested that the concentration technique of PK, and type A healing, both result in a physical and emotional draining of the psychic. This implies that some kind of energy-flow from the psychic is involved. For example, poltergeist effects obey the laws of energy transmission in the physical world – they centre upon one individual and fall off with increasing distance from that individual. But it is clear that no known energy could account for these effects, and we are forced to postulate a hypothetical 'psychic' energy as the cause of these events. LeShan admitted that he could not fit PK and type A healing into the Clairvoyant Reality framework. At present, I must reluctantly agree, and simply say that we cannot explain these effects.

In fact the other forms of PK are not much easier to explain. The 'relaxed' form might depend upon clairvoyance and precognition to some extent, but this is not a complete explanation. Once again, the view of a probabilistic future, with reality determined by the way we choose to look at the world, would seem to be the most likely explanation of, say, making a die fall with a particular face uppermost. (When you wish a die to fall with its six pip face upwards, you select one particular event from the infinite probabilities open to you, and turn it into reality – provided you are sufficiently close to the Clairvoyant Reality.)

As for metal-bending and table-moving, the most likely explanation seems to be that we can affect objects in the sensory world through our connection with them in the Clairvoyant Reality. Equating David Bohm's implicate universe with the Clairvoyant Reality makes this easier to understand. In this case, one would clearly be able to affect material objects by altering or directing the energy-flow from the implicate which gives them a particular form. This is, however, only a broad outline of an idea, and many questions remain unanswered.

The final category of psychic experience is also the most difficult to explain – type C healing. LeShan has suggested that it is necessary to propose a third framework of reality to explain both PK and type C healing. It is true that the subjective experience of a type C healing is noticeably different to that of any other psychic experience; whether or not this means that the events occur in a third framework of reality is another matter. However, it is interesting to note that many mystical traditions provide support for the suggestion, in that they centre on the idea of a progression of levels of development of the mind. If we are to postulate the existence of a third reality, we should also be able to identify a state of mind associated with that reality. Although I have no evidence to support the idea, it would not surprise me to learn that a person who had learnt to remain conscious while his brain was producing theta waves was working in a third reality. However, the idea need not concern us any more, because most of us only experience psychic work in the Clairvoyant Reality.

REFERENCES AND NOTES

1   A. Koestler, *The Roots of Coincidence* (Hutchinson, London, 1972) pp. 11–12.
2   Koestler, op. cit., p. 75.
3   Koestler, op. cit., p. 79.
4   Koestler, op. cit., p. 53.
5   Reported in Koestler, op. cit., p. 55.
6   F.A. Wolf, *Taking the Quantum Leap* (Harper and Row, New York, 1981).
7   Quoted in K. Pedler, *Mind Over Matter* (Eyre Methuen, London, 1981) p. 159.
8   See Wolf, op. cit.
9   L. LeShan, *Clairvoyant Reality* (Turnstone Press, Wellingborough, 1980), p. 27.
10 LeShan, op. cit., Chapter 3.
11 LeShan, op. cit., Chapter 4.
12 Quoted in LeShan, op. cit., p. 43.
13 LeShan, op. cit., p. 56.
14 Evelyn Underhill, *Practical Mysticism*; quoted in LeShan, op. cit., p. 58.
15 M. Planck, *Where is Science Going?*; quoted in LeShan, op. cit., p. 66.
16 L. Barnett, *The Universe and Dr Einstein*; quoted in LeShan, op. cit., p. 70.
17 H. Margenau, *The Nature of Physical Reality*; quoted in LeShan, op. cit., p. 71.
18 Quoted in LeShan, op. cit., p.72.
19 LeShan, op. cit., pp. 59–60.
20 I. Bentov, *Stalking the Wild Pendulum* (Wildwood House, London, 1978).

21   Ibid., p. 61.
22   LeShan, op. cit., pp. 107–8.
23   Quoted in LeShan, op. cit., pp. 111–12.

In Conclusion

The experiments described in this book should have enabled you to experience a wide range of psychic events. Even if you have not tried divination or dowsing, you may well have been convinced of the reality of telepathy, clairvoyance and precognition by the card-guessing experiments, the telepathic tests or the precognition dream-control method. To some readers, these events, and the way of viewing the world described in Chapter 14, will all represent new ideas and concepts. Others will have come across similar ideas before. But I believe that our constant search for a greater understanding of the psychic world – one which most of us intuitively feel 'is there', if only we could find it – means that the book contains something of interest to everyone. I have tried to avoid being dogmatic, for, as LeShan puts it, 'no one person can carry more than the smallest burden for opening new doors of understanding'; therefore, if you do continue your exploration of the psychic world, remember that; and remember also, that although you are stepping out along a path which has been well trodden before you, the journey will be as fresh and exciting for you as it was for the first person who made it.

Appendix

How to Calculate the Significance Level of Psychic Experiments

This requires a small amount of mathematics, but the calculations really are very simple.

1 *For any experiment where there are only two possible results,* you can intuitively grasp the principles by considering the fall of an ordinary, unbiased coin. (The analysis applies to any situation where there is an 'either/or' result, such as guessing whether the next card to be dealt from a pack will be red or black.) In 100 throws of the coin, we would expect heads and tails each to come down about 50 times by chance alone. But suppose a coin landed heads 59 times and tails 41, while you were trying to influence it to fall heads uppermost. Would this variation from the *expected* result (expected, that is, by chance alone) indicate that you have been working psychically, or is it merely an insignificant deviation from the expected result? A simple mathematical test provides the answer.* First, one writes down the result in a way that makes it easy to work out the maths.

- let the larger class of results – here, heads at 59 times – equal y
- let the smaller class of results – here, tails at 41 times – equal x
- work out the value of 'C'* from the following formula:

$$C = \frac{[(y - x) - 1]^2}{x + y}$$

---

* Mathematical purists who object to my adaptation of the Binomial formula will see that the adaptation does not alter the end result.

By substituting the values of 59 and 41, this becomes:

$$C = \frac{[(59 - 41) - 1]^2}{59 + 41}$$

therefore, $C = \dfrac{[18 - 1]^2}{100}$

$$= \frac{17^2}{100}$$

and so, $C = \dfrac{17 \times 17}{100} = \dfrac{289}{100} = \underline{2.89}$

Once you have calculated the value of C, you can look at the following table to calculate the probability (P) of your results *being due entirely to chance:*

When C =	2.7	3.8	6.6	9.5
P =	10%	5%	1%	0.2%
(approx.)	1 in 10	1 in 20	1 in 100	1 in 500

Thus, in our example, C, at 2.89, corresponds to a probability of between 5 and 10 per cent. What does this mean? The probability P is the probability that the difference between x and y is due to chance alone — in other words, that the results are insignificant, that they do not demonstrate a psychic effect. In this case, there is a probability greater than 5% (1 in 20), but less than 10% (1 in 10), that the results are due to chance. This could also be expressed in other ways:

- The observed difference between x and y is likely to occur by chance (with a frequency of) more than once in every twenty runs of the experiment.
- The odds against this result being due to chance are lower than 20 to 1.

You should really reject any result unless the odds against it having occurred by chance are 100 (or more) to 1.

2 *For any experiment where there are several alternative outcomes,* the situation is more complicated. Suppose first of all that you were trying to influence the fall of a die so that it landed

with its six pip face uppermost. Let us suppose that you were to throw it a total of sixty times. Obviously we would expect each face to land uppermost ten times by chance alone; that is the *expected* result. Hopefully, you would be able to influence the die so that it landed with 'six' upwards more than ten times. The results which you actually obtain constitute the *observed* results; here is an example of how you should record them.

FACE	1	2	3	4	5	6
Expected (E)	10	10	10	10	10	10
Observed (O)	7	7	11*	6	8	21*
(E — O)	3	3	1	4	2	11
$(E — O)^2$	9	9	1	16	6	121
$\dfrac{(E — O)^2}{E}$	$\dfrac{9}{10} = 0.9$	$\dfrac{9}{10} = 0.9$	$\dfrac{1}{10} = 0.1$	$\dfrac{16}{10} = 1.6$	$\dfrac{4}{10} = 0.4$	$\dfrac{121}{10} = 12.1$

* When 'O' is larger than 'E', (E — O) is simply the difference between them.

The next step is to add up all the values of $\dfrac{(E — O)^2}{E}$ in the bottom row of the table. Here the total is $0.9 + 0.9 + 0.1 + 1.6 + 0.4 + 12.1 = 16$. Let us call this total 'A'. You can look up the value of probability (P) which corresponds to 'A' in the following table (this table only applies to experiments with six possible outcomes):

When A =	9.2	11.1	15.1	20.5
P =	10%	5%	1%	0.1%
(approx.)	1 in 10	1 in 20	1 in 100	1 in 1000

With a value for 'A' of 16, the probability (P) of the results being due to chance alone is less than 1 per cent, or 1 in 100. To put it the other way, the odds against the result being due to chance alone are more than 100 to 1 — very strong evidence that a psychic effect is at work.

Let us suppose that you are trying to guess the design of Zener cards as they are turned over. Since there are five designs in the pack, you could expect to guess, on average, every fifth card correctly by chance alone. Thus, if you turned over 250 cards, you could expect fifty correct 'calls' by chance. This fifty would, assuming your guesses were random, be made up of equal numbers of each of the five designs. This, then, is the *expected* result (expected by chance alone, that is). You should write down the results you actually obtain, that is, the *observed* results, in the following way:

Design	☆	□	+	○	◇
Expected (E)	10	10	10	10	10
Observed (O)	12*	9	17*	14	18*
(E — O)	2	1	7	4	8
(E — O)²	4	1	49	16	64
$\dfrac{(E - O)^2}{E}$	$\dfrac{4}{10} = 0.4$	$\dfrac{1}{10} = 0.1$	$\dfrac{49}{10} = 4.9$	$\dfrac{16}{10} = 1.6$	$\dfrac{64}{10} = 6.4$

* When 'O' is larger than 'E', (E — O) is simply the difference between them.

(Note that the two experiments are rather different. With the die-throwing test, the total of numbers in the 'observed' row must equal the total in the 'expected' row. This is not true here, because one may guess correctly any number of cards between 0 and 250.) Once again, you add up the totals in the bottom row; here, this is 0.4 + 0.1 + 4.9 + 1.6 + 6.4 = *13.4*. We can represent this value with the letter 'A', and then use the following table to calculate the probability (P) that the results are due to chance alone (this table only applies to experimental investigations with five alternative 'choices'):

When A =	7.8	9.5	13.3	18.5
P =	10%	5%	1%	0.1%
(approx.)	1 in 10	1 in 20	1 in 100	1 in 1000

In this particular experiment, with the value of A at 13.4, the probability of the results being due to chance is just under 1 per cent, or 1 in 100. This strongly suggests that a psychic influence has been involved in the card guessing.

It is possible, as I mentioned in Chapter 6, to use an ordinary pack of cards and merely guess the suit. The following table gives the relevant values of 'A' and P:

When A =	6.2	7.8	11.3	16.3
P =	10%	5%	1%	0.1%
(approx.)	1 in 10	1 in 20	1 in 100	1 in 1000

(In all these tests, if the value of 'O' and 'E' are the same then $\dfrac{(E - O)^2}{E}$ will be equal to zero.)

So, what should you do if you think you are an exceptional psychic? There are a few scientists working in the field who might be interested to hear from you. Since their addresses tend to change rather frequently, you might be best advised to ask the British or American Societies for Psychical Research for advice or recent information. You can contact these societies, respectively, at:

> 1 Adam and Eve Mews
> Kensington
> London W8 6UG

and

> 5 West 73rd Street
> New York
> NY 10023.

Index